SEARCH THE SCRIPTURES

SEARCH
THE
SCRIPTURES

A systematic Bible study course

General Editor:
THE REV. ALAN M. STIBBS, M.A.
Oak Hill College, London

INTER-VARSITY FELLOWSHIP
39 Bedford Square, London WC1

© INTER-VARSITY FELLOWSHIP

First Edition in one volume 1949
Second Edition 1951
Third Edition (revised order of study) 1955
Fourth Edition 1960
Fifth Edition (completely revised) 1967

STANDARD BOOK NUMBERS:

One-volume edition (casebound): 85110 613 7
Part 1 (limp): 85110 562 9
Part 2 (limp): 85110 563 7
Part 3 (limp): 85110 564 5

Printed in Great Britain by
Staples Printers Ltd., at their Rochester, Kent, establishment

PREFACE

This course of Bible reading was first issued in 1934 in response to a widespread demand from Christian students and others for a systematic plan which could be used daily. Its aim is to guide the reader through the whole Bible in three years of regular daily study.

The General Editor of the original edition was G. T. Manley. In 1949 a new and revised course was prepared by H. W. Oldham and others. The present fresh and thorough revision has been undertaken by a large team of helpers, each of whom has worked on an allotted section. These include G. L. Carey, D. Catchpole, M. J. Cole, J. C. Connell, P. A. Crowe, A. E. Cundall, D. R. J. Evans, M. R. W. Farrer, P. K. Finnie, R. T. France, P. H. Hacking, A. R. Henderson, J. B. Job, Dr. and Mrs. A. Johnston, F. D. Kidner, G. E. Lane, Mrs. A. Metcalfe, H. Peskett, Mrs. M. Roberts, Miss E. M. Scheuermeier, J. A. Simpson, J. K. Spence, Miss M. Sugden, J. B. Taylor, Miss R. E. Wintle, D. R. Wooldridge and D. R. Wright; with A. M. Stibbs acting as General Editor.

As G. T. Manley wrote of the compilers of the earlier editions, all who have shared in preparing this revision 'know well the difficulty of sustained Bible study, and how many a hindrance Satan will put in the way. But they pray that the guidance here given may, by the grace of God, stimulate such a taste for His Word as to make the time daily spent upon it a delight as well as a source of strength'.

OVER-ALL PLAN OF THE COURSE

NEW TESTAMENT

Gospels

Letters

SUGGESTIONS ON METHOD OF STUDY

Aim of the course

The aim of this course is to help Christians young and old in their daily study of the Word of God. It differs from other schemes which have a similar aim in a number of important respects. First, the whole Bible can be covered in a period of three years. Second, the method employed is to set a number of questions on the content, meaning and application of each passage to be studied. These are designed to encourage a personal searching of the Scriptures to discover God's particular teaching and message for the reader from each portion of His Word. Third, explanatory notes are reduced to an absolute minimum on the principle that the truth which we dig out for ourselves is more likely to be remembered. There is real profit and enjoyment in wrestling with a difficult passage, as the many thousands who have already used the course can testify.

The right approach

The term 'Bible study' has been used to describe this course, but it is a phrase that needs some interpreting. We must not approach the Bible merely academically, as if it were some textbook we are required to read for an examination. We read and study our Bible because this is a means appointed by God by which we can encounter Him. It is vital that we seek the Lord, and desire to know His will as it applies to us. Otherwise, answering a question can become an end in itself and instead of a joyful meeting with our God our Bible study will become either a rather boring duty, or, at best, nothing more than an intellectually absorbing pastime.[1]

While it is true that in our study of the Bible we must use our minds, employing all the intellectual faculties which God has given us, our primary requirement is not intellectual but spiritual. The

[1] On this whole question of the right approach to personal Bible study and prayer see *The Quiet Time*, edited by J. D. C. Anderson (IVF, London; IVP, Chicago).

Bible itself declares: 'The unspiritual man does not receive the gifts of the Spirit of God, for they are folly to him, and he is not able to understand them because they are spiritually discerned' (1 Cor. 2: 14). Similarly, our Lord reveals in one of His prayers that the things of God are often hidden from those whom men reckon wise, and revealed to those He calls 'babes' (Mt. 11: 25, 26). Our approach to God's Word must be wholly without pride and self-confidence. We should begin with a humble acknowledgment of our dependence upon God, and a prayer that His Holy Spirit will open our blind eyes and give us spiritual discernment and understanding.

At the same time we must remember that God has been pleased to reveal His truth in documents written originally in ancient languages and in a particular historical environment. Consequently full discovery of all that God has to say to us through them demands diligent study involving patient and persistent enquiry and the use of all proper available aids to understanding. Bible study ought to be regarded, therefore, as demanding the serious and concentrated exercise of all one's intellectual powers. God rewards those who seek in order to find.

The time required

Those who originally planned *Search the Scriptures* had in mind people who would give at least twenty minutes a day to their personal Bible study. But experience over many years has shown that to get the maximum amount of help from the course rather longer than this may be required. Without it, prayerful meditation on the passage, which is a necessary preliminary to answering the questions, may well get curtailed. Those with little time to give would therefore be well advised to seek some slightly less demanding scheme as an aid to their Bible study.[1] But for those who can set aside, say, half an hour a day, experience has shown that this course can be of immense spiritual benefit. In addition, the question and answer method provides valuable practical training in how to study the Bible for oneself.

Arrangement

The full course can be completed in exactly three years by anyone who will keep at it and do the study each day without fail. This is the challenge it presents. But it is intended to act as a servant, not as a task master, to assist rather than to discourage. Obviously, illness

[1] For example, the introductory Bible study course, *Hold the Faith* (IVF, London; IVP, Chicago), which provides approximately six months' study.

or a change in circumstances may necessitate a change in routine. Others may find that they benefit by a move to another Bible study method for short periods. The important thing is to keep constantly before one's mind the aim of completing a personal study of the whole Bible, even though one finds it takes longer than the recommended three years.

The order in which it is suggested that the books of the Bible should be studied has been worked out with some care. There are both deliberate sequence and planned variety. Except where other considerations have demanded some different arrangement, Old Testament books are studied in their historical order. Since, however, 1 and 2 Kings are studied as part of this historical sequence, 1 and 2 Chronicles are inserted towards the end of the course as a final review of the history of the kingdoms of Israel and Judah.

Only where the study of a book occupies more than four weeks has its study been subdivided into sections to be taken with intervals in between. Studies which occupy the first year have been chosen to help the beginner. They contain, for instance, a much larger proportion of New Testament reading than is possible in the remainder of the course.

Those who are accustomed to reading only a short passage of Scripture each day may find the length of some of the Old Testament allocations rather forbidding. But there is much to be said for the practice of reading large sections (and even whole books) at a sitting. After all, this is what we usually do when reading for study or pleasure. With the time available, the detailed study of particular verses is less important than a broad, general acquaintance with the contents and main spiritual truths of the passage.

One big advantage of a course of this kind is that it can so easily be adapted to suit individual needs. For example, if the order of study recommended is not what the reader wants, it can very easily be altered. Again, the larger books of the Bible, which in this course are divided into sections, can, if preferred, be read without interruption in their entirety. Cross references are provided from the end of one section to the beginning of the next to make this simpler. If, on the other hand, it is preferred to break the books down into even smaller sections for the sake of variety, there is nothing to prevent the course being adapted in this way. Another suggestion is that readers may wish to increase the amount of New Testament study they do in the later stages of the course by turning again to some of the books studied in Part One. This will lengthen the time taken to complete the course but some may well decide that other considerations are more important.

To make this easier, the books are listed in their biblical order on pp. vi, vii and viii with the total number of studies allocated to each and the page where each section begins. But any deviation from the prescribed order ought not to be allowed to interfere with the ultimate aim of completing for oneself a study of the whole Bible.

A check-list on which each book or section can be ticked when completed appears at the beginning of each of the three Parts; and each individual study can also be ticked as it is done, in the small 'boxes' provided for the purpose.

Requirements

(a) *A Bible*

The course is based in general upon the Revised Standard Version of the Bible, and can naturally be used with this alone. There will be occasions when other translations may be helpful to the study of the passage; and there are, of course, numerous other versions of the Bible or New Testament available today. While care should be taken in their use (sometimes they are paraphrases rather than translations), they can often throw light on a passage that might otherwise be somewhat obscure.

(b) *A notebook*

This can be used both for rough notes made during the study each day and also for w iting up more carefully those findings which are felt to be of more permanent value. Some have found it wise to leave the recording of these notes to a later time when the value of the daily discoveries can be seen in perspective. In the initial thrill of discovery all sorts of things may be thought to be of great and lasting worth which will not appear quite so relevant a week later. The majority, however, will probably not have time to come back to each study in this way. A good loose-leaf book can serve for both purposes.

(c) *Other aids to Bible study*

A Bible and a notebook are the only two *essential* requirements, but the following reference books can be recommended as useful aids to Bible study.

(i) *The New Bible Commentary*.[1] A popular one-volume commentary on the whole Bible. Some explanatory notes and a certain amount of background information are provided in the course, but to have a commentary available for reference can be very valuable. If time is limited, however, such helps should be used only sparingly.

---

[1] IVF, London; Eerdmans, Grand Rapids, Michigan. See also the Tyndale Commentaries on individual books (Tyndale Press, London; Eerdmans, Grand Rapids, Michigan).

What is discovered personally from a study of the Bible will mean far more than what is read hurriedly in a commentary.

(ii) *The New Bible Dictionary*.[1] This contains a great deal of useful information concerning places, customs and the meaning of words and ideas. Again, care must be taken to see that the time set apart for personal study is not replaced by reading some of the fascinating facts recorded in the Dictionary! On the other hand, such a reference work can be a very helpful supplement to the study of the Bible.

Procedure

What follows is put forward merely as a suggestion for those starting the course. After a while, each individual will naturally wish to make his own adaptations of this procedure as seem best to him in the light of his experience.

1   Begin with prayer along the lines previously suggested.

2   Read the portion of Scripture appointed for study. It is best not to read the questions before reading the Bible passage itself. Knowing what the questions are may mean that one's interest becomes limited too soon to those particular points.

3   Read the questions and any notes on the passage. Think about the passage in the light of the questions asked. Then try to work out the answer to these: they will be found a very useful aid to concentration.

4   Write answers to the questions in the notebook. The user of the course is strongly advised to discipline himself to do this, and not just to pass over the questions with a vague idea that they have been answered. Greatest profit will be derived from actually committing to paper what has been discovered from the passage. At the same time it is possible to be too dependent on the questions. Especially in the larger Old Testament sections the questions set obviously do not exhaust the meaning of the passage. The reader may even feel that at times they miss what is to him the main point of the passage or jump to application too quickly. Fair enough! If readers find themselves wanting to formulate their own lines of inquiry instead of being tied to the questions set, one of the aims of the course is being achieved.

Some users of the course may wonder at times whether their answer to a question is in fact the one intended! This does not really matter provided that scriptural teaching is being better understood. But where other Scripture references are provided for comparison these will often indicate the kind of answer expected. But it is better to concentrate first on getting an answer from the verses

[1] IVF, London; Eerdmans, Grand Rapids, Michigan.

set for study, and to leave the references to other Scriptures until that has been done. The temptation to study the cross references rather than the passage set must be avoided.

It can also be very helpful to have a weekly review of the ground covered, and of the outstanding truths which have been learnt or more fully appreciated.

Some people may find that all this gives them too much to do in the time they have allocated to Bible study. In that case an attempt could be made to adapt the course so that only one question is dealt with each day, concentrating on the one which seems likely to be the most profitable. Then move on to the next study. To do otherwise means that the course may well take six years or even longer to complete. When it is only occasionally that one finds there is not enough time to finish, it may well be possible to complete the study later in the day or at the weekend, while the reading is still comparatively fresh in the mind.

Where more than two questions are provided for the same study, the third (or fourth) question is to be regarded as an optional extra; or as an alternative to the first two; or for possible use when the same Bible passage is studied later. One of the advantages of a course of this kind is that it can be used repeatedly.

5   Use the passage as a basis for worship and praise. Pray over the lessons learnt. There will be some particular thought (or thoughts) which is God's word to you for the day. Seek to discover it, and then in prayer relate it practically to your own life. Remember that God's inspired Word has been given to us for an essentially practical purpose; to teach us, to reprove us, to correct us, to instruct us in righteousness, and to make us spiritually mature and equipped for every good work (2 Tim. 3: 16, 17).

ABBREVIATIONS

Books of the Old Testament: Gn., Ex., Lv., Nu., Dt., Jos., Jdg., Ru., 1, 2 Sa., 1, 2 Ki., 1, 2 Ch., Ezr., Ne., Est., Jb., Ps. (Pss.), Pr., Ec., Ct., Is., Je., La., Ezk., Dn., Ho., Joel, Am., Ob., Jon., Mi., Na., Hab., Zp., Hg., Zc., Mal.

Books of the New Testament: Mt., Mk., Lk., Jn., Acts, Rom., 1, 2 Cor., Gal., Eph., Phil., Col., 1, 2 Thes., 1, 2 Tim., Tit., Phm., Heb., Jas., 1, 2 Pet., 1, 2, 3 Jn., Jude, Rev.

AV	Authorized Version (1611)
ICC	*International Critical Commentary*
LXX	Septuagint Version (*i.e.*, translation of the Old Testament into Greek, *c.* 250 BC)
mg.	margin
Moffatt	*A New Translation of the Bible* by James Moffatt (1935)
NBC	*The New Bible Commentary* (2nd ed. 1954)
NBD	*The New Bible Dictionary* (1962)
NEB	The New English Bible: New Testament (1961)
RSV	Revised Standard Version (1946–52)
RV	Revised Version (1885)
TNTC	*Tyndale New Testament Commentaries*
TOTC	*Tyndale Old Testament Commentaries*
Way	*Letters of St. Paul and Hebrews* by Arthur S. Way (1921)
Weymouth	*The New Testament in Modern Speech* by R. F. Weymouth (1902)

PART TWO

Check-list of material contained in this part (tick when completed):

LEVITICUS

Introduction

The third book of the Pentateuch was referred to by the Jews in various ways—the 'priest's law', 'priest's book', 'law of the offerings' —for Leviticus consists mainly of ritual law. The author is not named in the book. All we know is that it was given by divine revelation at Sinai in the time of Moses.

Leviticus is a book of great significance from many points of view. It provides us with a background to all the other books of the Bible. It helps us to understand references to sacrificial offerings and cere-monies of purification, or institutions such as the sabbatical year or the year of jubilee. Orthodox Jews have to this day found their binding regulations, their food laws, for instance, in this book. But it also shows us the way in which the God of Israel combats sin in Israel: first by means of His institutions of sacrifice and purification (social sin by means of the sabbatical year and year of jubilee, sexual sins by means of the laws of chastity) and second, by means of His promises and warnings. All this is of interest to Christians as showing the principles of atonement and purification applied in a particular context. In doing so it is natural that there should be many illus-trations of the work of the Lord Jesus Christ. His atoning death on the cross is the reality of which the rituals of Leviticus are but pictures and symbols.

Analysis

☐ **STUDY 1   Leviticus 1**

God is now dwelling in the midst of His people, and gives them directions concerning their worship of Him and their communion with Him. Notice how throughout this book God is the speaker, through Moses.

1   What are the two outstanding features of the burnt offering mentioned here? See, *e.g.*, verses 3, 9, 10, 13.

2   What significance would the burnt offering have for the person making the offering? See, *e.g.*, verses 4, 9, 13, 17.

☐ **STUDY 2   Leviticus 2 and 3**

1   The cereal offering represents a blameless life. The purity of its ingredients is emphasized (see 2: 1, 11). The worshipper who is not blameless draws near to God with acceptance in the power of an offering possessing the perfection which he lacks. Consider how this offering is fulfilled in Christ. *Cf.* Heb. 7: 26; 1 Jn. 2: 6.

2   The peace offering speaks of communion, based on the blood of atonement (3: 1, 2), and expressed in a whole burnt offering pleasing to the Lord (3: 5). Do you know the heart-satisfaction of such a relation to God?

☐ **STUDY 3   Leviticus 4: 1 – 6: 7**

1   What is it that distinguishes the sin and guilt offerings from the burnt, meal, and peace offerings? See 4: 2, 13, 22, *etc.* Of what divine provision for our need are we here assured? *Cf.* Lv. 17: 11.

2   Notice particularly what was done with the body and with the blood of the sacrifice in the sin offering (4: 6, 7, 11, 12). How do these solemn ordinances indicate God's hatred of sin, and suggest some of the fearful results that may arise out of sin?

Note. The sin and guilt offerings have much in common, but the sin offering had reference rather to the person of the offender in his guilt towards God, whereas the guilt offering was an atonement for the offence especially in its relation to man. Hence the sin offering differed for different classes of persons (4: 3, 13, 22, 27); and in the guilt offering the guilty party, in addition to his offering, had also to make amends for the wrong done (5: 16; 6: 4, 5).

☐ **STUDY 4   Leviticus 6: 8 – 7: 38**

Distinction must be made between public and private offerings. In addition to the private burnt offerings of the people, there was a daily, public burnt offering morning and evening. *Cf.* Ex. 29: 38–42. It is this daily sacrifice that is referred to in 6: 9, 12, with directions that the fire must not be allowed to go out on the altar.

1   Neither the sacrifice nor the fire was to fail. What lessons can we learn from that? *Cf.* Heb. 6: 11, 12.

2 7: 11–21. In the peace offering the people offered to God the spontaneous gifts of their love. What were the three kinds of peace offerings which individuals might bring? What about us? *Cf.* Heb. 13: 15, 16.

Note. A 'wave offering' (7: 30) means an offering or part of an offering presented to the Lord by waving it towards Him, before receiving it back from Him. In a 'heave offering' (7: 32) the word 'heave' does not mean to throw, but to lift or take off, and indicates the part of the offering taken off for the priests.

☐ STUDY 5 Leviticus 8

Cf. Ex. 29: 44. The directions for the ceremony were given in Ex. 28 and 29; this chapter gives the account of it.

1 What is the order in which the dedication of priests and Tabernacle took place? Do you see any significance in this order?

2 In the sacrifice of the ram of ordination (*i.e.,* of dedication to special service), what special use was made of the blood? What symbolic significance does this have? *Cf.* Rom. 6: 13.

☐ STUDY 6 Leviticus 9 and 10

The Tabernacle and priests have been sanctified and dedicated; all was now ready for the normal work of the priesthood to begin.

1 What was Aaron's first offering at the start of his ministry? Though pardoned, anointed and consecrated, he still needed mercy through atoning blood. But when all was duly offered, how did God show His acceptance of His people's worship? With 9: 22a, *cf.* Nu. 6: 22–27.

2 What did Nadab and Abihu do? What happened? Why did God act like this?

Notes
1 10: 1. 'Unholy fire': this may mean fire not taken from the altar, but the central thought is that it was fire which God had not authorized.
2 10: 8–11. It has long been thought that Nadab and Abihu may have been indulging in wine; hence this prohibition.
3 The significance of 10: 16–20 seems to be that Aaron realized that Nadab and Abihu had taken part in the offering of the sin offering and that this rendered it unacceptable and unclean. This is a touching story of Aaron's full acceptance of God's verdict on his own sons.

☐ STUDY 7 Leviticus 11

1 What would the distinction between clean and unclean teach Israel about God and His worship? See verses 44, 45. Consider the

great changes in their habits that the coming of God to dwell among them brought about. *Cf.* I Pet. I: 14–16; Eph. 4: 22–24.

2 How did our Lord show that such distinctions are not now binding? What constitutes defilement in God's sight? *Cf.* Mk. 7: 14–23.

☐ **STUDY 8   Leviticus 12: 1 – 13: 46**

I Did the mere fact of being born a Jew give a child a place in the covenant? See 12: 3, Note I below, and Dt. 10: 15, 16; 30: 6. How do the principles illustrated here apply today?

2 From chapter 13 trace some of the parallels that exist between the plague of leprosy and the plague of sin.

Notes
I   12: 3. Circumcision had a twofold significance, namely, identification with God's covenant people, and purification from unfitness for such a role.
2   12: 8. *Cf.* Lk. 2: 22–24.

☐ **STUDY 9   Leviticus 13: 47 – 14: 32**

I If leprosy is an illustration of sin, what is the general teaching of 13: 47–59 regarding sin-contaminated habits and practices?

2 What is the significance of the fact that the leper had to be healed before he was cleansed from the defilement of his leprosy? *Cf.* Jn. 3: 3; Gal. 6: 15.

☐ **STUDY 10   Leviticus 14: 33 – 15: 33**

I How does this portion show that sin, wherever found and in whatever form, is defiling in God's sight, and prevents acceptance before Him?

2 Chapter 15 is usually taken to represent the defilement of secret sin. Notice (a) how it pollutes the whole life and all around it, and (b) that this kind of defilement requires atonement just as much as other forms of sin. *Cf.* Pss. 19: 12; 51: 6–9.

☐ **STUDY 11   Leviticus 16**

I Sketch out the order of the ceremonies of the Day of Atonement.

2 What do you learn from this chapter about (a) the conditions of approach into God's presence; (b) the complete removal of sin's guilt through substitution; (c) the necessity on man's part of submission in penitence and faith to God's way of salvation?

Note. Verses 8, 10, 26. 'Azazel' means 'destruction'. This goat, upon which the lot fell for destruction, is referred to in the AV as the 'scapegoat', a term with which we are more familiar.

☐ **STUDY 12   Leviticus 17**

There are two main instructions in this portion: first, that all domestic animals which are to be killed shall be brought to the Tabernacle (verses 3–9); and second, that no blood must be eaten (verses 10–16). The former of these instructions points to a time when animals were not killed except in connection with worship of some kind.

1   What would this first instruction (verses 3–9) teach Israel about God? Where is it suggested in these verses that this instruction is directed against idolatrous worship?

2   Why was the eating of blood so strictly forbidden? See verse 11 in particular. What is the significance of this for us?

☐ **STUDY 13   Leviticus 18**

In chapters 18–20 we pass from the worship of the people to their behaviour. Chapter 18 prohibits unlawful marriage, unchastity, and Molech worship; but the last is dealt with more fully in 20: 2–5.

1   What reasons are given for Israel's obedience to these laws and how important is this obedience? See verses 1–5 and 24–30.

2   What light is thrown by this chapter upon God's command for the extermination of the Canaanites?

☐ **STUDY 14   Leviticus 19 and 20**

1   What particular attribute of God receives emphasis in these chapters as a ground of obedience to His commands? *Cf.* 1 Pet. 1: 14–17.

2   Which one of the ten commandments do these laws elaborate? What significant summary of the law of God is to be found here?

Note. Molech was the national god of Ammon. Great cruelty seems to have been associated with worship of him. Children were offered in sacrifice and burned with fire. Hence God's implacable opposition to all such worship.

☐ **STUDY 15   Leviticus 21 and 22**

1   What words and expressions occur frequently, giving the reason why these instructions are imposed? List some ways in which we ought to be showing similar concern.

2   What can we learn here about the serious effects on our Christian lives of things which are apparently small, but spiritually unclean?

☐   **STUDY 16   Leviticus 23**

1   List the feasts and note the general character of each. What did they have in common? And what were their differences?

2   What are the New Testament parallels to the three main feasts and what is the significance of each? (a) The Passover. *Cf.* 1 Cor. 5: 7, 8. (b) The Feast of Weeks, or Pentecost. *Cf.* Acts 2: 1–4. (c) The Feast of Tabernacles, the final ingathering of the harvest. *Cf.* Rev. 7: 9, 10.

Notes
1   Verse 11. The sheaf of the first-fruits of the barley harvest waved on the morrow after the sabbath points to Christ's resurrection. *Cf.* 1 Cor. 15: 23.
2   Verse 16. 'Fifty days': hence the name 'Pentecost', *i.e.*, the 'fiftieth' (day).
3   Verse 17. 'Two loaves of bread to be waved': the first-fruits of the wheat harvest, representing the church of Christ in its first beginnings (Jn. 12: 24).

☐   **STUDY 17   Leviticus 24**

1   Consider the significance of the words 'pure' and 'continually' which recur in verses 1–9. Apply these words to your own worship and Christian service.

2   What attributes of God's character are set side by side in this chapter? *Cf.* Heb. 10: 19–31. What constraint should such awareness put upon us?

☐   **STUDY 18   Leviticus 25**

1   How was the year of jubilee reckoned, and what was its general purpose? Are there any corresponding spiritual blessings in Christ? And how may we enjoy them? *Cf.* Gal. 2: 4; 5: 1, 13.

2   What light is shed in this chapter on the principles governing our relationship to God and to one another in Christ? See especially verses 17, 23, 35, 36, 38, 42, 43, 55.

☐   **STUDY 19   Leviticus 26**

1   What spiritual blessings are promised to obedient Christians, corresponding to these promised here to an obedient Israel?

2   What are the reasons for punishment and the conditions for restoration given here? How do these apply in the Christian life?

☐ STUDY 20   Leviticus 27

Instruction as to what is to be done where an offering has been made to the Lord and the giver wants to redeem it; also a regulation about tithes.

1   What can be redeemed and what cannot be redeemed? What does this teach us about the seriousness of vows made to God? Is there any exception to the statement in verse 29? *Cf.* Ps. 49: 7–9, 15; Mk. 10: 45.

2   What does this chapter show of the Lord's character? What does He require in His people?

THE LETTER TO THE HEBREWS

Introduction

The Epistle is an exhortation and warning to Jewish believers to continue in the faith of Christ and not to fall back into Judaism. Christ is set forth as the fulfilment of Old Testament type and prophecy, and the faith and endurance of the Old Testament saints are held up as examples to believers. Needless to say, the teaching of the Epistle has a scope and value far beyond what was of immediate concern to Jewish believers of the first century. It shows the new covenant, of which Jesus, the Son of God, is Mediator, to be not only far superior to the first covenant, but the final and perfect religion, both as regards revelation (1: 1 – 2: 18) and redemption (3: 1 – 10: 18). The Epistle also contains practical teaching concerning life under the new covenant. It constitutes a divine call to all who have professed themselves Christians to see that their faith is a reality, and to continue in it, and a very definite challenge to those who have not yet put their faith in Christ. It sets forth Christ very fully in His capacity as our High Priest, shows His divine nature, and yet points out the reality of His humility and suffering as man in a way no other book does in the whole Bible, the Gospels not excepted.

Analysis

1: 1 – 2: 18   Christ the perfect Revealer, better than angels (a) as the Son of God (1: 5–14); and (b) as the Son of man (2: 15–18).

3: 1 – 10: 18   Christ the perfect Redeemer, better than Moses (3: 1–6) and better than Aaron (a) in His Person and character (4: 14 – 5: 10); (b) in the 'order' of His priesthood (7: 1–25); and (c) in His ministry (8: 1 – 9: 12) and in His offering (9: 13 – 10: 18).

10: 19 – 12: 29   Practical teaching.

13: 1–25   Final counsels and greetings.

Within this outline are contained five passages of solemn warning:

2: 1–4   Against the danger of drifting.

3: 7 – 4: 13   Against the danger of missing God's promised rest.

5: 11 – 6: 20   Against the danger of losing salvation.

10: 26–39   Against the danger of drawing back.

12: 25–29   Against the danger of refusing to hear God's final word.

☐ **STUDY 1   Hebrews 1**

1   Verses 1–4. List the statements made about Christ in verses 2 and 3. What do these statements tell us about His Person and work? In what ways is He greater than prophets and angels?

2   How do the scriptures quoted in verses 5–14 confirm the statement of verse 4? Define for yourself the ways in which what God says of Christ is different from what He says of angels.

Notes
1   The emphasis laid upon Christ's superiority to angels, which to us seems obvious, is explained by the fact that, to the Jews, one of the chief glories of the Old Testament revelation was that it was given through angels. See 2: 2.
2   Verse 7. Angels are created beings; they are God's servants; and their form and appearance suffer change and transformation at God's pleasure. Contrast the royal dominion and unchanging being of the Son (verses 8–12).

☐ **STUDY 2   Hebrews 2**

1   Verses 1–4. Why ought we to 'pay the closer attention to what we have heard' (verse 1)? Sort out the reasons here stated. Against what practical dangers is this warning directed?

2   What, according to the Scriptures (*e.g.*, Ps. 8), is man's divinely-intended destiny? How do we here see God's purpose for man being brought to its fulfilment? What path did the Son of God have to tread to make it possible for sinful men to share in this fulfilment? What, in consequence, can He now do for us?

☐ **STUDY 3   Hebrews 3: 1–6**

1   Verses 1, 6. Christians are here described as those who confess Christ and respond to His call. If these activities are to be fully meaningful, we must 'consider Jesus' as our 'apostle and high priest'. What, then, can Christ do for us, and what does He demand from us as (a) our Apostle, and (b) our High Priest?

2   Verses 2–5. Find three ways in these verses in which Christ is said to excel Moses.

Notes
1   Verse 1. As 'Apostle' Jesus was sent from God to men to reveal; as 'High Priest' He offered Himself for men to God to redeem and to reconcile. *Cf.* 1: 1, 2a, 3b; 2: 3, 17; 4: 14; 5: 1; 8: 1.
2   Verses 2–6. 'God's house': this refers to God's people or household, not to the Tabernacle or Temple. Now it is we Christians who are God's house. Our heavenly calling makes us 'holy brethren' in God's family (verse 1).

☐ **STUDY 4   Hebrews 3: 7 – 4: 13**

1   3: 7 – 4: 2. What is the danger against which we are here warned? Why were the Israelites overtaken by it in the wilderness? How may we avoid similar disaster?

2   4: 1–13. In what ways does God use His Word in His dealings with us? What promise of His still stands open for our enjoyment? What are the conditions of obtaining its fulfilment in our experience? Can any avoid having dealings with Him?

Note. 3: 12, 13; 4: 1. In each of these verses an exhortation is addressed in the plural to the many, exhorting them all to take care lest any single one of their number fall away.

☐ **STUDY 5   Hebrews 4: 14 – 5: 10**

1   4: 14–16. What truths concerning our Christian High Priest are we here exhorted to confess, and what consequent privileges open to our enjoyment are we here exhorted fully to possess?

2   5: 1–10. What qualifications for high priesthood are set forth in verses 1–4? How are these possessed by Christ at a higher level and in a fuller way than could ever be true of a Levitical priest? What benefit can He consequently make ours, and on what condition?

Notes
1   The order of treatment in 5: 1–4 is reversed in 5: 5–10. The three points dealt with are (a) function, (b) understanding sympathy, (c) appointment to office.
2   5: 3. Every Jewish high priest was 'bound to offer sacrifice for his own sins'. Contrast 4: 15. Jesus was sinless.
3   5: 7–9. These verses give an amazing insight into our Lord's true humanity and earthly humility.

☐ STUDY 6   Hebrews 5: 11 – 6: 8

1   5: 11–14. What is the writer's complaint about his readers? What does he imply are the conditions of spiritual growth? By these standards, considering how long I have been a Christian, by this time what ought I to be?

2   6: 1–8. What teaching constitutes the foundation of the gospel? See Acts 2: 38; 20: 21; 26: 18. What reason is given here for not laying this foundation again? What were the only possibilities now open to such people?

Notes
1   5: 11. As the writer is about to begin his exposition of the Melchizedek priesthood of Christ, he is arrested by a sense of the difficulty of expounding it to those who have become spiritually so dull of hearing.
2   5: 14. Note the practical evidence of maturity. *Cf.* Is. 7: 16.
3   6: 4–8. To understand these verses compare the writer's earlier reference to the Israelites in the wilderness. It was impossible for Moses to take them back into Egypt, and to bring them out through the Passover and the Red Sea a second time. Either they must go on with God and enter in, or come under God's judgment, and be finally shut out. See 3: 10–12.

☐ STUDY 7   Hebrews 6: 9–20

1   Verses 9–12. What gives the writer confidence concerning his readers' final salvation? In what ways does he desire to see improvement in their Christian living? Examine yourself to see in which of these characteristics you are strong or weak.

2   Verses 13–20. If we have made Christ our refuge, what three unshakable grounds of assurance have we that our confidence and hope will not disappoint us? In what ways is Jesus Himself like an anchor? What benefits does He guarantee?

Notes
1   Verses 10–12. Note the mention of love, hope and faith. *Cf.* 1 Thes. 1: 3; 5: 8.
2   Verse 12. 'Sluggish': in 5: 11 the same Greek adjective is translated 'dull'. Other renderings are 'lazy' or 'slothful'.
3   Verses 11, 12. 'Until the end'; '. . . and patience'. This is an emphasis typical of this letter. *Cf.* 3: 14; 6: 15; 10: 35, 36.

☐ STUDY 8   Hebrews 7: 1–14

1   Verses 1–10. On what grounds is Melchizedek said to be greater than Abraham and consequently superior to the Levitical priesthood? By what the scriptural record both does and does not tell us about him, in what ways is Melchizedek made to resemble the Son of God?

2 Verses 11–14. Why could not Jesus possibly be a priest after the order of Aaron? What does the promise in the Old Testament of a new order of priesthood (see Ps. 110: 4) imply concerning the existing Levitical priesthood? If the priesthood is changed, what must inevitably be changed as well?

Notes
1 Verse 1. 'This Melchizedek, king . . . priest': among the Israelites these two offices were never held by the same person.
2 Verse 2. 'First . . . righteousness, and then . . . peace': *cf.* Is. 32: 17.
3 Verse 12. The priesthood was so fundamental to the old covenant between God and His people, that any change in the order of priesthood must of necessity involve a change in the whole constitution; *i.e.*, it implies nothing less than an accompanying new, and indeed better, covenant. See 7: 22.

☐ **STUDY 9** **Hebrews 7: 15–28**

1 Verses 15–25. What are the distinctive differences between the Levitical and the Melchizedek orders of priesthood—in qualification for office, in continuance in office and in efficacy? In relation to Christ's office what is added by God's oath?

2 Verses 23–28. How do these verses show that in Jesus we have a perfect High Priest, and that He perfectly meets the sinner's need? In what ways is He unique both in Person and work?

Note. Verse 25. 'For all time': the Greek phrase means 'to the uttermost' both of time and of degree: 'completely' (RV mg.).

☐ **STUDY 10** **Hebrews 8**

1 Verses 1–6. Jews were used to seeing Levitical priests fulfil their ministry in an earthly sanctuary. As Christians they needed to appreciate that Christ's ministry is different and 'much more excellent' (verse 6). In what ways is this true? What is the significance of His being already seated at the right hand of God's throne (verse 1)? *Cf.* 10: 10–14; 4: 14–16; Eph. 4: 8.

2 Verses 7–13. Why did the first covenant fail? Was there anything wrong with it? In contrast to it, in what ways does the new covenant meet our need, give us 'better promises' (verse 6), and make success certain?

Note. Verses 10–12. Experimental progress into the enjoyment of the blessings of the new covenant is best appreciated from the bottom to the top as (a) forgiveness of sins, (b) personal knowledge of the Lord, (c) covenant relation to Him, (d) the indwelling Spirit turning the external restraint of the law into an internal constraint to do God's will.

☐ **STUDY 11   Hebrews 9: 1–15**

1   Verses 1–10. In what respects did the earthly sanctuary and its ceremonies come short, and for what reasons?

2   Verses 11–15. In what ways is the ministry which Christ fulfilled superior to, and more effective than, the Levitical ceremonies? List its far-reaching consequences.

Notes
1   Verse 9. 'Perfect the conscience': *i.e.*, free it from guilt and defilement, or 'purify' it (verse 14).
2   Verse 12. The Greek does not say that Christ took blood into God's presence, like the Levitical high priest took blood into the inner shrine (verse 6). Rather He entered 'through' (see RSV mg.) His own blood, *i.e.*, on the ground of His death or shed blood. For by this the veil had been rent which shut men out. *Cf.* Mk. 15: 36, 37; Heb. 10: 19–22.

☐ **STUDY 12   Hebrews 9: 15–28**

1   Verses 15–23. What are the reasons why Christ's death was necessary? Of what benefits can we be sure because it has occurred?

2   Verses 24–28. What differences are here indicated between what the Jewish high priest did and what Christ has done? What are the consequences of Christ's one sacrifice of Himself? How can it affect what happens to us when this life is over?

Note. Verses 15–22. According to ancient practice covenants were sealed in blood, by the symbolic introduction of the death of the parties making it. Also, once a transgression of a covenant obligation had been committed, death became necessary for a second reason, to pay the penalty of such failure. So 'without the shedding of blood there is no forgiveness of sins' (see *NBC*, p. 1103).

☐ **STUDY 13   Hebrews 10: 1–18**

1   Write down as many contrasts as you can find between the sacrifices of the Tabernacle and the sacrifice offered by Christ. Why did the latter succeed where the former failed?

2   What consequences of Christ's sacrifice (a) are enjoyed by Him, and (b) can be enjoyed by us?

3   To what truths does the Holy Spirit bear witness in the Old Testament passages which are here quoted?

Notes
1   Verses 5–9. The truth emphasized here is that a moral act of personal obedience has superseded ritual ceremonies, which in themselves had no inherent worth. They were only 'a shadow of the good things to come' (verse 1).

2 Verses 1, 10, 14. 'Perfected' and 'sanctified': the meaning is that by Christ's one sacrifice we are brought for ever into a perfect, unalterable relationship of acceptance with God and consecration to His service. No further offering for sin is necessary (verse 18).

☐ **STUDY 14   Hebrews 10: 19–39**

Having finished his doctrinal exposition, the writer proceeds to give practical counsel for the life we are to live under the new covenant.

1   Verses 19–25. How are we here exhorted to give expression to our faith, hope and love? Seek in your own life to discern ways in which these exhortations demand your obedience.

2   Verses 26–39. For those who have God-given light concerning the way of salvation, what is the only alternative to going on with God? Why are its consequences so serious? On what grounds does the writer here expect, and appeal for, the best from his readers?

Notes
1   Verse 22. As the high priest and his sons at their consecration for service in the earthly sanctuary were washed with water and sprinkled with the blood of sacrifice (Ex. 29: 4, 21), so we in 'heart' and 'body' (that is, inwardly and outwardly, in our whole being) have been 'sanctified' by Christ's sacrifice.
2   Verses 26, 29. The writer has in mind deliberate and persistent apostasy— self-chosen denial and defiance of both the Son of God and the Spirit of grace. The closing words of verse 26 mean that no second atoning sacrifice is provided for those who reject the sacrifice of Christ and His sanctifying blood.

☐ **STUDY 15   Hebrews 11: 1–22**

1   Faith deals with things unseen and things future, and, in particular, with the living God and His faithful doing (verses 1, 6). It is sure of the present reality of the one, and of the coming fulfilment of the other. Notice in detail how these characteristics of faith were exhibited in the lives of the individuals here mentioned. What does this teach me I need to covet if my life is to please God?

2   Verses 7–16. To what should faith in God take heed, and what does its full expression involve? Where is the crowning fulfilment of its hopes to be enjoyed? How should such awareness affect my present outlook, action, and attitude to life?

3   Verses 17–19. What apparent contradiction was involved (as Abraham at first saw it) between God's promise and God's command concerning Isaac? How did Abraham's faith in God triumph over this test, and what new hope did Abraham have in God?

☐ **STUDY 16   Hebrews 11: 23–40**

1   Verses 23–28. Note how Moses' faith gave him the twofold awareness and assurance emphasized in verse 1. What choices did

such faith lead him to make (a) concerning the world in which he had grown up, and (b) concerning the cost of siding with the Israelites? How ought similar faith to affect my attitude towards the interests to which I choose to devote my life?

2 Verses 28–31. What different steps and stages of faith and its expression are illustrated by these four instances? What kind of faith did the capture of Jericho demand? *Cf.* 3: 14; 6: 11, 12; 10: 35, 36. Is my faith at all weak in this last quality?

3 Verses 32–40. These verses give a summary of the achievements and the sufferings of the men and women of faith. Note that the victories are of all kinds; and that the most outstanding witness is given by the 'martyrs' who suffered and died rather than deny their faith. In what ways am I more privileged than they? Would I be ready to follow their example, or does their faith put mine to shame?

☐ STUDY 17   Hebrews 12: 1–17

1 Verses 1–4. What quality does the Christian race particularly demand? What conditions must be fulfilled if it is to be run successfully? How may I gain the help I need to finish my course?

2 Verses 5–11. For what purpose does God in His providence order some of the earthly experiences to His children? What goal has He in view for us? Upon what kind of response from us does our full enjoyment of benefit depend?

3 Verses 12–17. What dangers beset those who are spiritually slack and careless? How may a whole group be affected by one renegade? What practical steps to avoid these dangers are here (either explicitly or implicitly) given?

☐ STUDY 18   Hebrews 12: 18–29

1 Verses 18–24. List the ways in which our Christian privileges under the new covenant excel the experiences of the Israelites at Sinai. Of what ought we by faith deliberately to be conscious when we draw nigh to God through Christ and His shed blood?

2 Verses 25–29. What is here said to be impending and inescapable? How do we know this? *Cf.* Mk. 13: 31; 2 Pet. 3: 9–14. How, in consequence, ought we to live our present earthly lives?

Notes
1 Verse 23. 'The assembly of the firstborn': *i.e.*, the church (Greek, *ecclesia*) of the privileged who have a heavenly inheritance and whose names are written in heaven. *Cf.* Lk. 10: 20; Rev. 21: 27.
2 Verse 23. 'The spirits of just men made perfect': *i.e.*, either Old Testament saints, or all the faithful departed.

☐ **STUDY 19   Hebrews 13: 1–8**

1   List in detail the various aspects of Christian duty which are here enjoined or implied. Examine your own life and circumstances in order to discover ways in which your practical obedience is demanded.

2   Verses 5, 6, 8. What makes the Christian adequate to face every possible circumstance? Why is there for him nothing to fear, and no-one who can really harm him? For his encouragement what use may he make of the Old Testament Scriptures?

3   Verse 7. In what ways should Christian leaders, whose life on earth has ended, be remembered?

Note. Verse 1. 'Continue': *cf.* 6: 10; 10: 32–34.

☐ **STUDY 20   Hebrews 13: 9–25**

1   What decisive choice and action are here demanded of the first readers of this Epistle between their old Jewish associations and their new Christian allegiance? What comparable choices do those who wish to follow Christ still have to make today?

2   Verses 15, 16, 20, 21. What may we count on God to do for us, and why? What is the purpose in view? What sacrifices may we now offer in God's service? How far is this purpose finding fulfilment in my life?

☐ **STUDY 21   Revision**

1   Review the doctrinal teaching of this Epistle. See the Introduction and Analysis. List the ways in which what is ours under the new covenant is better than the things which the Israelites enjoyed under the old covenant. What do we have to do to gain full possession of these benefits? Why is rejection of them so serious?

2   Consider the positive exhortations to be found in the following passages: 2: 1; 4: 1, 11, 14, 16; 6: 1; 10: 22–24; 12: 1, 28; 13: 17, 22. Which of these exhortations do I particularly need to heed, and to act upon?

NUMBERS

Introduction

In the book of Numbers the narrative of Israel's journey from Egypt, interrupted at the foot of Sinai (Ex. 19) for the giving of the law, is resumed. The history, however, is throughout the book alternated with further laws and enactments. The book is a story of failure. The people are brought to the edge of the promised land, but owing to unbelief and disobedience are prevented from entering it. Then follows the long forty years of wandering in the wilderness, passed over almost in silence, except for one or two incidents. Finally, the people come again to Kadesh-barnea, the whole generation that came out of Egypt as adults being dead, with three exceptions. Their first conquests are recounted, and their destiny foretold in the mysterious prophecies of Balaam.

Analysis

1 – 4	Numbering and order of the tribes. Work of the Levites.
5, 6	Various civil and religious laws.
7 – 9	Dedication of the Tabernacle. Observance of the Passover.
10 – 12	Journeyings and complaints.
13, 14	The spies are sent into the land. The people refuse to go forward.
15	Religious laws.
16, 17	The rebellion of Korah.
18, 19	Laws concerning the Levites and concerning purification.
20, 21	Approach to the land and conquest of the Amorite kings.
22 – 25	Prophecy of Balaam, and sin at Baal-Peor.
26	Numbering of the tribes.
27 – 30	Various civil and religious laws.
31	Conquest of the Midianites.
32	Inheritance of the two and a half tribes.
33, 34	Statistics.
35, 36	Various civil and religious laws.

☐ **STUDY 1   Numbers 1 and 2. Numbering and order of the tribes**

1   Israel's immediate future was to be characterized by war and worship. How is this shown in chapter 1? Can the two be separated in the daily life of the Christian? Cf. 2 Cor. 10: 3–6; Eph. 6: 10–13.

2   What point is there in the detailed ordering of the tribes as given in chapter 2? What are the central and governing interests? Cf. 1 Cor. 12: 7, 11, 12; 14: 40.

☐ **STUDY 2   Numbers 3 and 4. Work of the Levites**

For background details concerning the tribe of Levi, see Ex. 6: 16–25; 32: 25–29; Lv. 10.

1   How was the work assigned to the Levites divided between the three 'families' of the tribe? How, if at all, might the command 'each to his task' (4: 49) apply to Christians? Do these two chapters throw any light on the possible implications of such a command? See especially 3: 5–10, 25, 31, 36, 45; 4: 46–49.

2   Whom did the Levites represent? Why did the first-born belong to God? What does 'redemption' mean in this context? Is there a New Testament counterpart which involves us?

3   How does 4: 1–20 bring out the 'frighteningly' sacred character of the Tabernacle? Cf. 1: 51b, 53; 2 Sa. 6: 6–11; Rev. 4: 8. What truths does this illustrate and enforce?

☐ **STUDY 3   Numbers 5: 1 – 6: 21. Civil and religious laws**

Many of the civil and religious laws of Israel and the rites connected with them are hard for us to understand. They may seem strangely abhorrent, sometimes inhuman or quasi-magical in character. It is important to bear in mind (a) the authority of the priest in every sphere of Israel's life, including that of cleanliness and hygiene, which were as much a part of 'religious' ceremony as the worship in the Tabernacle; (b) the background of religious rites common to the whole of the ancient Near East and used by Israel, though transformed both by her faith in the one true God, and in order to make them usable in His worship; and (c) the need that this new, God-chosen nation should be constantly reminded of the holiness and moral demands of her God.

1   What sort of people were to be 'put out' of the camp, and why? Cf. Lv. 13: 46; 15: 31. What interests of humanitarian justice are satisfied in the commands of 5: 11–31? These seem like purely magical rites, but note verses 16, 18, 21 and 30.

2   How did the Nazirite's separation to God find expression? What was the point of it all, since it was apparently *not* an act of service

which could be offered to God as acceptable in and of itself apart from the regular offerings of the Tabernacle? See 6: 14–16; and *cf.* Lv. 1–7 for details. How far is there a similar challenge to consecration confronting the believer in Christ? *Cf.* Heb. 9: 10–14; Rom. 12: 1, 2.

Note. 6: 2. A 'Nazirite' was a man who desired for a period to set himself apart for God in an unusual way. The Hebrew root, *nazir*, expresses the idea of separation or consecration.

□ STUDY 4 Numbers 6: 22 – 7: 89. Dedication of the Tabernacle

1   What did it mean for Aaron and his sons to 'put' God's name 'upon the people of Israel'? How did the blessing effect this? See Dt. 28: 9, 10; Dn. 9: 18, 19; and *cf.* 1 Cor. 6: 11; 2 Cor. 13: 14.

2   Notice how often the words 'offering' or 'dedication offering' are used in chapter 7. The solemnity is emphasized by repetition. In what way is 7: 89 a fitting climax to this 'build-up'? What did it all mean to Israel? Do *we* 'offer' to God in this atmosphere of reverence? What similar climax may we expect when we thus approach God? *Cf.* Heb. 3: 7; 4: 16.

Note. 6: 26. 'Peace' (Heb. *shalom*) does not mean simply 'cessation of hostility'. It indicates 'completeness', 'perfection' or 'well-being'.

□ STUDY 5 Numbers 8: 1 – 9: 14. Observance of the Passover

1   Chapter 8 is a re-assertion of the 'separatedness' of the Levites. How was this made clear to Israel? What is a wave offering? *Cf.* Lv. 10: 15; 23: 20; a probable meaning is 'contribution'. What was the relationship of the Levites to God, priests and people respectively?

2   9: 1–14. How is the importance of the Passover shown here? *Cf.* Ex. 12: 24–27. What are we to learn from this?

3   What do we see here of Moses' way of exercising leadership? How did he deal with practical problems when individuals brought them to him?

□ STUDY 6 Numbers 9: 15 – 10: 36. The journeying begins again

1   Israel were made very sure of God's guidance. Without the actual symbols of cloud and fire can we claim the same assurance? *Cf.* Acts 16: 6–10; Rom. 8: 14. Why the repetition of the words 'at the command of the Lord'?

2 Notice the correspondences *and* the differences between 10: 14–28 and 2: 3–31. What is there in chapter 10 to show that, although God led and protected the children of Israel, He did not expect them to be utterly passive and to do nothing for themselves?

3 What was the significance of the trumpets (10: 1–10)? *Cf.* Lv. 23: 24; Nu. 29: 1. It has been said, 'When God remembers, He acts'. *Cf.* Gn. 8: 1; 19: 29; 30: 22.

Note. 10: 35, 36. These were the words uttered publicly by Moses at the beginning and end of each day's journey. Note their expression of dependence upon God's protection and desire for His abiding Presence.

☐ **STUDY 7 Numbers 11 and 12. Complaints**

1 What different attitudes are shown here by the people, the rabble, Joshua, Miriam and Aaron, and Moses? How does Moses stand out as 'different'?

2 How did God 'deal' with the various complaints made?

Note. 12: 3. 'Meek': not concerned for his own interests or prestige, and so able to pay no attention to the unfair attacks upon himself.

☐ **STUDY 8 Numbers 13: 1 – 14: 10a. The spies are sent into the land**

1 To what places in Canaan did the spies go? Look up Hebron and the Valley of Eshcol on a map. What were they commissioned to discover, and what report did they give?

2 What lay behind the opposing views expressed in 13: 30 and 31? Were Caleb and Joshua being unrealistically optimistic and refusing to face facts? What was the outcome of the people's fear and unbelief? Notice how *few* believed, and the frequent occurrence of the word 'all' in 14: 1–10. *Cf.* Heb. 4: 1, 2.

Note. 13: 32. 'A land that devours its inhabitants': this probably refers to the constant wars between its people, and their ferocity in internecine strife.

☐ **STUDY 9 Numbers 14: 10b–45**

1 What can we learn from Moses' prayer, especially concerning governing motives and grounds of appeal to God?

2 Although forgiven, the people suffered the consequences of their sin. How? In what way do they show themselves throughout this story (Nu. 13 and 14) to be typical of us?

☐ **STUDY 10   Numbers 15. Religious laws**

1   What do verses 1–21 teach us about making offerings which are pleasing to God?

2   Why was there no way of atonement for the person who sinned 'with a high hand'? What does this mean? *Cf.* Mk. 3: 28, 29; Heb. 10: 26–31, 39; Ps. 19: 13.

3   Notice by whom the deliberate law-breaker had to be dealt with and in what way. *Cf.* Mt. 18: 15–17; 1 Cor. 5; Heb. 12: 15. Why is such church discipline so little practised?

Note. Verse 38. 'Tassels': these were made of twisted thread and attached by a blue ribbon to the robe, to remind the wearer of the commandments of the Lord, and of his obligation to keep them.

☐ **STUDY 11   Numbers 16: 1–35**

1   There is evidence here of a double revolt: one by Korah (a Levite) 'and all his company' against Moses and Aaron; and one by Dathan and Abiram (Reubenites) against Moses. What was the ground of complaint in each case? See 16: 3 and 16: 13; 14. To what extent was it justified? *Cf.* Heb. 5: 4; 2 Cor. 10: 18.

2   What lay behind the revolts which made them serious enough to warrant so drastic a punishment and warning to the people? See especially verses 11, 19, 28, 30.

Note. Verse 1. That such men should lead an open revolt against the authority of Moses and Aaron meant that it was a very serious outbreak of discontent.

☐ **STUDY 12   Numbers 16: 36 – 18: 7**

1   How is the exclusive Aaronite priesthood strengthened and confirmed? What does the service of the priesthood involve? Notice especially 16: 48, and compare the work of Christ as great High Priest. *Cf.* Heb. 5: 1, 9, 10; 7: 25–28; 9: 11, 12, 26.

2   How could our service be transformed by thinking of it as a gift (18: 7)? *Cf.* 1 Tim. 1: 12–14; 2 Tim. 1: 6.

☐ **STUDY 13   Numbers 18: 8 – 19: 22**

1   What does 18: 8–32 teach us about offerings which are holy and belong by right to God?

2   What are the special features of the sacrifice described in 19: 1–10? Note the use to which the ashes were put (19: 9, 12, 17–19). What are the 'dead works' from which we need to be purified?

Notes

1 18:19. 'A covenant of salt': *i.e.*, an indissoluble covenant. *Cf.* 2 Ch. 13:5.
2 19:9, 12, 17-19. The cleansing virtue of the sacrifice already made was
thus symbolically stored up and applied, as need arose, to the unclean. *Cf.*
Heb. 9:13, 14; 1 Jn. 1:7-9.

☐ **STUDY 14   Numbers 20**

1 Notice Moses' and Aaron's reaction to the people's discontent
(verse 6). What did God desire to achieve through this incident?
See verses 6, 8, 12. How did Moses and Aaron fail, and in what
terms is their failure described? See verses 10, 12, 24; *cf.* 27:14;
Dt. 32:51.

2 God's anger with Moses and Aaron may at first seem to us out
of proportion to the extent of their failure. What ought we to learn
from this? What ought we also to learn from the fact that even
'meek' (12:3) Moses 'spoke words that were rash' (Ps. 106:33)?

☐ **STUDY 15   Numbers 21. Conquest of the Amorite kings**

1 Israel's reaction to adversity gets a little monotonous (verse 5),
and it is easy to say, 'Why cannot they learn to trust God?' But are
not we often as unbelieving? Notice how Jesus uses this story
(verses 6-9) as a 'type' in Jn. 3:14, 15. What parallels are there in
the condition of the afflicted and in the means of salvation in each
case? Why a serpent on the pole? *Cf.* 2 Cor. 5:21.

2 It is worth tracing Israel's journey on a map from 20:1 onwards.
Notice how circuitous it was. What evidence is there, as *against*
20:2, 3 and 21:4, 5, that Israel *was* learning trust and obedience
through discipline? What discipline? *Cf.* Dt. 8:2.

☐ **STUDY 16   Numbers 22. The story of Balaam**

This is a difficult story. Before tackling it, it will probably be helpful to read
2 Pet. 2:15, 16; Jude 11; Nu. 31:16 and Rev. 2:14, which give a clue as to
Balaam's true character and motives.

1 Balaam's influence and relationship to God are interesting. Think
about them. Consider also Moab's fear in the face of Israel's advance.
What does this show concerning the ways in which God works?

2 What was the 'chink' in Balaam's armour? Why did his
'guidance' seem all confused after that? Contrast verse 12 with
verses 20, 22, 32, 35. What ought we to learn from his failure? Do
you think Rom. 14:22b, 23 and 1 Tim. 6:9, 10 give us a similar
warning?

☐ STUDY 17 Numbers 23 and 24 (first study)

1 Two studies are to be given to these chapters. On this occasion concentrate attention on Balaam's oracles. Make a list of the statements in them which indicate God's special purpose for, and care of, the people of Israel.

2 Seek to appreciate the full significance of each one of these statements. What were the grounds of Balaam's assurance of Israel's victory and success? What similar grounds have we for thankfulness and wonder? *Cf.*, *e.g.*, 1 Pet. 2: 9, 10.

Note. 23: 10. 'The righteous': the word is plural, and refers here to the Israelites.

☐ STUDY 18 Numbers 23 and 24 (second study)

1 What can we learn from Balaam about the demands of being a spokesman for God, and a steward or minister of His Word? Note carefully the answers which Balaam gives to Balak's suggestions. *Cf.* 1 Cor. 9: 16, 17.

2 23: 19. What is here said to make God's words different in character from those of men? When God gives us His word, of what else can we be sure? *Cf.* 1 Thes. 5: 24.

☐ STUDY 19 Numbers 25 and 26

1 Chapter 25. Why was God's anger so fierce against the sins of His people? *Cf.* 1 Cor. 10: 6–12. In this situation what two complementary concerns stirred Phinehas to action? Who likewise was moved to action on our account by similar concerns?

2 Chapter 26. Compare the numbering in chapter 1. This is a new generation. See verses 64, 65. Notice which tribes had increased and which decreased. What explains the survival of Caleb and Joshua?

Note. 25: 1–5. Nu. 31: 16 and Rev. 2: 14 reveal that these developments were due to Balaam's activities. The Israelites were seduced into idolatry and immorality.

☐ STUDY 20 Numbers 27 and 36. Laws of inheritance

1 What was the principle lying behind the request of the daughters of Zelophehad, and to what did the request lead? What was the importance of all this?

2 What was Moses' overriding concern before his death? How was Joshua's commission different from that of Moses? Was it inferior?

☐ **STUDY 21   Numbers 28 and 29. Review of Israel's sacrifices**

1   Distinguish between the daily sacrifice throughout the year offered every morning and evening (28: 3–8) and the additional sacrifices: (a) on the sabbath (28: 9, 10); (b) at the new moon each month (28: 11–15); (c) throughout the feast of unleavened bread and at the Passover itself (28: 17–25, see Note below); (d) at the Feast of Weeks (28: 26–31); (e) at the blowing of trumpets (29: 1–6); (f) on the Day of Atonement (29: 7–11); (g) at the Feast of Tabernacles (29: 12–38).

2   It was easy for these sacrifices to become mere ritual—so much so that later prophets strongly condemned their misuse. Am. 5: 21–24 and Is. 1: 11–18 give a clue as to the purpose of these offerings and to God's real requirements in and through them. *Cf.* also Heb. 10: 1–18.

Note. 28: 24. The meaning is that the sacrifices prescribed above in verses 19–22 are to be offered daily throughout the feast.

☐ **STUDY 22   Numbers 30**

1   How does this chapter show our responsibility in speech? *Cf.* Mt. 5: 33–37; 12: 36.

2   Do you think the woman's relationship to father and husband should be viewed as merely local Israelite custom, or is there an implied principle which holds in the twentieth century too?

☐ **STUDY 23   Numbers 31. Conquest of the Midianites**

1   This is another difficult passage unless you bear in mind (a) that it records only the bare outline of an event far greater in scope; (b) that it is recorded from a particular standpoint (the Midianite account was probably quite different from this one); and (c) that its message concerns a God of love who *must* purge of evil everything that is His. What are the forms of purging found in this account? In what directions ought a Christian to act with comparable severity? *Cf.* Col. 3: 5–11.

2   What does the chapter teach about sharing and giving? On what grounds were portions given to the priests and Levites?

☐ **STUDY 24   Numbers 32. Inheritance of the two and a half tribes**

1   What was wrong with the request of Reuben and Gad? What was the result which Moses feared might arise from it, and on what

conditions only could it be granted? Why is this event particularly significant for Israel as it arrives in the promised land, and begins to form itself into a tribal confederacy? How will its future life as a 'nation' differ from all that it has been up to now?

2 What great principle with regard to sin and its consequences is expressed in verse 23? Can you think of instances in Scripture which illustrate its working? *Cf.* Gal. 6: 7, 8.

Note. Verses 1-5. The tribes of Reuben and Gad understandably thought that the land of Jazer and Gilead would suit their large herds of cattle. But their self-willed choice brought their descendants into constant trouble in later times. The territory lacked natural frontiers and was somewhat isolated and exposed to attack. Often in later centuries the other tribes had to come to their rescue. *Cf.* 1 Sa. 11; 1 Ki. 22: 3.

☐ **STUDY 25   Numbers 33 – 35**

1 What details stand out in this statistical account which make one aware of the particular interests and concerns of Moses (see 33: 2) the 'statistician'? What does he want his readers to take note of and remember?

2 The theme of entry into a promised inheritance appears several times in the New Testament. *Cf.* especially Acts 20: 32; Rom. 8: 17; Gal. 3: 29; Heb. 6: 11, 12. Heb. 11 makes it clear that our *real* inheritance, both Israel's and Christians', is a heavenly one. What does Israel's entry into its earthly inheritance teach us about preparing for and claiming our true inheritance? To what warnings ought we to pay heed?

3 What can we learn from chapter 35 concerning God's standards of judgment as regards manslaughter and murder?

Note. For consideration of Numbers 36, see Study 20 above.

MARK 1 - 9

Introduction

It is generally held that this Gospel was written by John Mark, the nephew of Barnabas, and is the earliest of the four Gospels. According to tradition it is based upon the teaching of the apostle Peter, whose interpreter Mark became (*cf.* 1 Pet. 5: 13), and was written in Rome for the church there. It begins with a short preliminary statement of John the Baptist's ministry, and of the baptism and temptation of Jesus, and then passes on to His public ministry in Galilee. In common with the other Gospels, it devotes a comparatively large space to Jesus' sufferings, death and resurrection.

The story centres in the confession of Peter, 'Thou art the Christ' (8: 27–29). Up to that time it tells of our Lord's activity in preaching and healing; but after the confession of Peter, Jesus makes known to the Twelve that He must suffer and die, and be raised the third day, and His face is turned towards the cross. The disciples failed to understand; and the work of Jesus in this latter half of the Gospel consists largely in teaching His disciples, and seeking to wean them from the false ideas of the kingdom which possessed their minds.

The closing verses of the Gospel (16: 9–20) do not appear to be the original ending. Some ancient manuscripts end at 16: 8, and others have a different paragraph at the close. But these verses contain the great missionary commission and have an established claim to be regarded as a part of Scripture.

Analysis

☐ **STUDY 1   Mark 1: 1–15**

1 Why 'the gospel' (verse 1)? How is this record different from a biography? What blessings of the gospel of Christ were anticipated in the Baptist's preaching? *Cf.* Acts 2: 38. When Jesus Himself preached 'the gospel of God' what aspects of its accomplishment and enjoyment did He stress?

2 Observe how the Father, Son and Holy Spirit are all active in the events recorded—and Satan also. What does this imply concerning the issues involved in the coming story and in our own earthly lives?

Note. Note Mark's significant use of the description 'gospel'. It is of such 'good tidings' that Isaiah had explicitly written. *Cf.* Is. 40: 9-11; 52: 7-10; 61: 1-4.

☐ **STUDY 2   Mark 1: 16–34**

1 In what different ways does Jesus here exercise His authority? What kind of questions did such actions make people ask? On what did they repeatedly focus attention?

2 How were these Galilaean fishermen to become personal soul-winners? What were the conditions and the cost of the realization of such a surprising suggestion? Is there any reason why a similar change could not happen in my life?

Notes
1 Verse 22. The scribes quoted the great authorities. Jesus spoke as if He Himself were the supreme authority. *Cf.* 'But I say to you' (Mt. 5: 21, 22, 33, 34).
2 Verses 25–27. Jesus did not invoke God's Name like Jewish exorcists. He spoke as if the decisive authority was His own; and it 'worked'. The unclean spirits obeyed *Him*.

☐ **STUDY 3   Mark 1: 35 – 2: 12**

1 After the astonishing events of the preceding day Jesus had to consider what He should do next. How did He arrive at a decision,

and to what decision did He come? In what way did the healed leper's disobedience hinder Jesus' work? What bearing has this upon (a) our prayer life, and (b) the church's missionary duty? *Cf.* Jn. 20: 21; Mk. 16: 15.

2 What evidences do you find in this story in chapter 2 of our Lord's powers of discernment? What did Jesus 'see'? And when He confirmed a verbal claim, which men questioned, by a miraculous work, which none could deny, to what truths was He bearing decisive witness?

Note. 2: 4. The house would have a flat roof, which could be reached by an outside stairway (*cf.* 13: 15).

☐ **STUDY 4   Mark 2: 13 – 3: 6**

1 Note how, when questions were asked about His behaviour, Jesus made Himself and the work which He had come to do the sufficient justification for His action. *Cf.* 2: 6–12. What claims was He thus making for Himself?

2 Why did not Jesus' disciples stand condemned for 'doing what is not lawful on the sabbath'? Who did stand condemned for their wrong use of the sabbath in the subsequent controversy concerning the healing of the man with a withered hand? Since Jesus used the sabbath as His day, and for men's good, how ought we to use the Lord's day?

Notes
1 2: 19. The 'bridegroom' is, according to Old Testament usage, virtually a description of God in His covenant relation to His chosen people Israel. *Cf.* Ho. 2: 16–20.
2 2: 25, 26. Note the repeated phrase 'those who were *with him*'. In such company their action could not be condemned.
3 2: 23, 24 and 3: 2. The scribes taught that to pluck ears of corn was a form of *reaping* which the law did not allow on the sabbath (Ex. 34: 21); also that it was unlawful to do the work of healing on the sabbath, *unless life was in danger.*

☐ **STUDY 5   Mark 3: 7–19a**

1 At this stage in His ministry, what obvious dangers and what positive desires made Jesus withdraw and go up into the hills? Whom did He take with Him, and why? What were the over-riding aims and the underlying strategy of His method?

2 The Twelve are first described as 'disciples' (*i.e.*, 'learners') and later as 'apostles' (see 3: 14, mg.; *i.e.*, 'men sent on a mission'). What kind of response did each calling demand? Can we become one without becoming the other? How far have you got in this sequence?

☐ **STUDY 6   Mark 3: 19b–35**

1   Note the official source and the evil character of the opposition which Jesus now had to meet. His reply to their accusation falls into three parts: (a) He disproves their assertion; (b) He sets forth the true explanation of His power over evil spirits; (c) He gives a solemn warning. State His argument in your own words.

2   Jesus here distinguishes His spiritual kinsmen from His human relatives. Why did the latter misunderstand Him? How do the former reveal their kinship with Him?

Notes
1   Verses 19b–21 are connected with verses 31–35. The words 'his friends' in verse 21 mean literally 'they from His home', and might be translated 'His family'.
2   Verses 29, 30. The scribes' sin was unforgivable because it was a defiant rejection of God-given light. They were knowingly calling good evil and holy unclean.

☐ **STUDY 7   Revision: Mark 1–3**

1   What strikes you most about Jesus in Mark's picture of Him at the beginning of His ministry? Of what truths was Jesus most concerned to make people aware? In other words, what is the essence of 'the gospel of God' which He preached?

2   What different kinds of reaction and result did the activity of Jesus provoke? To which class of people was Jesus prepared to give most? What must I be prepared to do to belong to this class? What may I then expect Him to give me?

☐ **STUDY 8   Mark 4: 1–20**

1   What does this parable teach concerning (a) the reasons why even the teaching of Jesus failed to produce fruit in the lives of many of the hearers; (b) the method by which the kingdom comes in this present age; (c) the criteria by which true success is measured in gospel preaching?

2   'He who has ears to hear, let him hear.' Is the Word of God finding entrance into my heart (verse 15)? Is it taking deep root (verses 16, 17)? Am I allowing some other crop to mature in my heart (verses 18, 19)? What measure of fruit is being produced in my life (verse 20)? *Cf.* Heb. 3: 7, 8.

Notes
1   A new method in Jesus' teaching begins here. The first parable is itself an indication of the purpose of teaching by parables. See verse 13. Such a method brings hearers under judgment, and finds out the truly responsive.

The real cause of blindness to the truth is unwillingness to repent and to be forgiven. Those who, as disciples, are responsive are given fuller understanding. See verse 34.

2 Verse 11. 'The secret' or 'mystery' (AV and RV): this is not something which cannot be understood. Rather it is something specially disclosed by divine revelation to those who are ready to understand it. 'The secret of the kingdom of God' is the content of the gospel of Christ. *Cf.* Eph. 3: 4; 6: 19.

☐ **STUDY 9   Mark 4: 21–34**

1 Verses 21–25. What is the responsibility of the hearer (a) for what he does with his knowledge, and (b) for his personal response to what he hears? What therefore are (a) the divinely intended consequences of spiritual privilege, and (b) the conditions of spiritual progress? *Cf.* Mk. 3: 14.

2 Verses 26–29. What is suggested in this parable concerning the character and purpose of (a) the first coming, and (b) the second coming into the world of the Lord Jesus? *Cf.* Ps. 126: 6. What truth do both of the parables here illustrate concerning the seed of God's word when it is sown in human hearts?

Note. Verses 26, 30. 'Kingdom': this word (particularly its Old Testament antecedent) signifies primarily 'sovereignty', *i.e.*, the sway exercised by a king, and only secondarily 'realm', *i.e.*, the sphere or territory over which he rules. 'The kingdom of God is as if . . .' (verse 26) virtually means 'the way God exercises His sway and works out His purposes among men is like this'.

☐ **STUDY 10   Mark 4: 35 – 5: 20**

1 4: 35–41. What were the disciples surprised at in Jesus, and what was He surprised at in them? What was He both testing and teaching by leading them into such an experience? Why did this miracle mean more to them than anything which they had yet seen Jesus do?

2 5: 1–20. Contrast men's way of treating the demoniac with what Jesus did for him. In which way is the power of evil active in my life being dealt with?

3 Why did the people 'beg Jesus to depart' (5: 17) and why did Jesus leave the healed demoniac behind? What may be the best form of witness in a home or neighbourhood that seems not to want Christ?

Notes
1 4: 40. It is significant that Jesus did not rebuke men used to sailing on the Sea of Galilee for their failure to bring Him safely through the storm.
2 5: 1–20. This happened in Decapolis, on the south-east side of the lake, in Gentile territory. The use of the title 'Most High God' (verse 7) and the local keeping of swine (verse 11) confirm this.

☐ **STUDY 11   Mark 5: 21 – 6: 6a**

1   These three incidents all emphasize the same necessity for any who would enjoy the experience of Christ's saving power. What is it? Why is it sometimes lacking? What must it resist?

2   Why were the disciples puzzled by the question of Jesus (5: 30, 31)? Why did Jesus wait for a trembling woman to speak in public before a crowd? What had she to give which no-one else there possessed? Do you possess it, and are you giving it—particularly before people who think that contact with Christ makes no difference?

Note. 5: 30, 31. 'Who?': this word is in the singular, *i.e.*, 'What one person?'

☐ **STUDY 12   Mark 6: 6b–30**

1   What can we learn (a) from our Lord's method of preparing His disciples for the work which He intended them later more fully to do, and (b) from such details as 'two by two', 'to take nothing for their journey' (*cf.* Mt. 10: 10), 'enter a house' and 'stay there', 'if . . . they refuse to hear you', 'they . . . preached that men should repent'?

2   How would you sum up Herod's character? What were the causes of this failure?

Note. 6: 7, 30. Another new beginning—the first mission of the Twelve; and so, when they return to report, they are temporarily called 'apostles' or 'missioners'.

☐ **STUDY 13   Mark 6: 30–56**

1   What lessons did the disciples need to learn before Christ could use them in feeding the crowd? Are there similar lessons we need to learn before we can be of use to Him?

2   Verses 45–53. It seems from the situation described here that the disciples got into difficulty as a result of obedience to Christ's command. What light does this throw upon the life of discipleship with its trials and deliverances? Why does it say in verse 48 'He meant to pass by them'? *Cf.* Lk. 24: 28, 29.

Note. Verse 48. 'The fourth watch': *i.e.*, the last watch, beginning about 3 a.m.

☐ **STUDY 14   Mark 7: 1–23**

1   No-one would dispute the earnestness of the Pharisees in observing genuine historical traditions, aimed at the honouring of God.

Why then should Christ use such strong language in condemning them (verse 6), and how does He show up their inconsistency?

2 Notice in verses 21–23 that Christ makes no distinction between sins of thought and sins of deed; they all alike defile a man. *Cf.* Mt. 5: 28. Are we seeking deliverance from the uncleanness of an evil heart? Or, like the Pharisees, are we content with a fair appearance outwardly?

3 Verses 17, 18a. Why do you think the disciples were so slow to understand some of Christ's simplest teaching? Are we perhaps also at fault here? If so, what ought we to do about it? *Cf.* Jn. 14: 26.

Notes
1 Verse 3. 'The tradition of the elders': *i.e.*, rules and regulations drawn up by past generations of scribes to guide people how to act. The Pharisees were those who made it their aim to walk strictly according to this 'tradition'. They regarded themselves, and were regarded by others, as 'the righteous'.
2 Verse 6. 'The Lord here both quotes Scripture and adds to it, thereby interpreting it' and establishing His own authority (see *Mark* (*TNTC*), p. 118).

☐ **STUDY 15   Mark 7: 24–37**

1 Why did Jesus at first seem to refuse the woman's request (*cf.* Mt. 15: 24), and why did He use such harsh words? What can we learn from her response, and from the Lord's answer to her further plea?

2 Assuming that the deaf and dumb man knew little or nothing about Jesus due to his limitations, what would the strange actions of Jesus mean to him? How would they help him to respond in faith?

3 Is there anything we can learn here about personal witness from the example of those who brought their deaf and dumb friend to Jesus?

Note. Verse 27. The term 'dogs' is an expression of contempt and disgust. In many parts of the East the dog is still basically a scavenger and by its very nature unclean and a potential carrier of disease (see *NBD* article: 'Dog').

☐ **STUDY 16   Mark 8: 1–26**

1 What characteristic features in the Lord Jesus stand out in the miracle of 8: 1–9? What special claim had this particular crowd on the Lord's provision? *Cf.* Mt. 6: 33. Of what was His provision a sign?

2 Why did Christ warn the disciples to beware of the leaven of the Pharisees and of Herod (verse 15)? Why did He question them about

the miracles that had recently taken place? How do thought and reflection of this kind help us to grow spiritually?

3 Verses 22-26. What may we learn from this incident about the way and the cost of leading someone in need to experience the saving power of Christ?

Note. Verse 15. The word 'leaven' used here symbolically refers to the unseen pervasive influence of sin.

☐ **STUDY 17 Mark 8: 27-38**

1 Verses 27-29. What did the disciples need to understand first of all, before Jesus could begin to explain to them about His death? Why was this so important, and why were most people so slow to understand it? *Cf.* Lk. 10: 21, 22.

2 Why was Peter unable to accept Christ's teaching about His death? What is the meaning of Christ's rebuke? In this matter of a right attitude to Christ's death, on whose side are you?

3 Verses 34-38. What two alternative courses are presented to us in these verses? Why is it so important to make the right choice? What does this involve, and what does Jesus say will be the final result of a wrong choice?

Notes
1 Verse 33. 'Get behind me, Satan!' Jesus was faced with a similar temptation in the wilderness to avoid the cross. *Cf.* Mt. 4: 8-10.
2 Verse 34. For the meaning of the word 'deny', see Lk. 12: 9; 22: 34. Here it means to disown self, to refuse to recognize the claims of self as against those of Christ.

☐ **STUDY 18 Mark 9: 1-29**

1 Verses 1-8. What would be the significance for the three disciples of the appearance of Moses and Elijah and also of the voice out of the cloud? *Cf.* Jn. 1: 45; Lk. 24: 27. How would this new experience be likely to help and encourage them?

2 Verses 11-13. What question did the scene on the mountain raise in the minds of the disciples, and how did Jesus reply? Consider how closely John the Baptist resembled Elijah.

3 Why was Jesus so disappointed at what He found on His return to the rest of the disciples? What does this incident teach us about the chief causes of failure in our Christian witness and service (see verses 23 and 29)?

Note. Verse 24. 'I believe; help my unbelief!' This implies, 'Help me just as I am, a doubter who wants to believe.'

☐ **STUDY 19   Mark 9: 30–50**

1   Verses 33–37. How does Jesus explain the way to become spiritually great? What especially ought we to learn from the example of a little child? *Cf.* Mt. 18: 4.

2   Verses 38–41. What three reasons does Jesus give here why the disciples should not have acted as they did? Why did they fail to gain similar understanding about His teaching concerning what was going to happen to Him (verses 30–32)?

3   Verses 43–48. What spiritual truth is Jesus seeking to convey here? In what sense are we to cut off a foot, or pluck out an eye? Why may it be necessary to apply such drastic measures?

Notes
1   Verses 44, 46, 48. 'Gehenna' (Greek) is a reference to the Valley of Hinnom outside Jerusalem, where the refuse of the city was cast and burnt. It had become a synonym for 'hell', *i.e.*, the place of final ruin and destruction.
2   Verse 49. 'Salted with fire': subjected to a fiery process of discipline to purge out corruption. *Cf.* 1 Pet. 4: 17; Heb. 12: 11.

For Studies 20–35 on Mark's Gospel see p. 189.

DEUTERONOMY

Introduction

The book of Deuteronomy finds the people again on the threshold of the land after the forty years of wandering. Moses, who is about to lay down his great task, addresses them before his death. The book consists chiefly of his addresses. Naturally, there is much matter repeated from earlier portions of the Pentateuch and, just as naturally, it is generally in a rather different form. Laws that were promulgated in the wilderness are adapted for use in the land. New matter, such as that relating to the central sanctuary and the setting up of the kingdom, is introduced. Finally, Moses, after solemn warnings to the people, appoints his successor, and ascends Mount Nebo to be laid to rest by God.

Analysis

1–3   Moses reviews the events of the past 38 years, proving to them God's faithfulness to His people in spite of their disobedience and unbelief.

4–11   Moses appeals to the people to render obedience to God as the only guarantee of a happy life in the promised land.

12–26   Moses outlines in detail the code of laws which God is giving them to observe in the land. These fall into three main categories: religious (12: 1 – 16: 17); civil (16: 18 – 18: 22); social (19–26).

27–30   Moses resumes his appeal for obedience to these laws, emphasizing this by foretelling the blessings or cursings that would come upon the people according to their manner of life. All this is set out in the form of a covenant (29, 30).

31–34   The end of Moses' life and ministry, including his instructions to Joshua (31); his great hymn to God (32); his blessing on the tribes (33); and the account of his death and burial (34).

☐ **STUDY 1   Deuteronomy 1**

1   The burden of this chapter is the people's sin in refusing to go forward to the promised land. How is the sin described (see verses 26, 27, 32) and what made the guilt of it greater (see Note on verses 9–18; also verses 31–33)?

2   What solemn lesson is taught in verses 40–45? Cf. Is. 59: 1, 2; Je. 11: 14; Heb. 12: 17.

3   What does this chapter teach us about the importance of knowing history, especially Bible history? Cf. Pss. 78: 1–8; 44: 1–8; 1 Cor. 10: 6–13; Rom. 15: 4.

Note. Verses 9–18. These verses seem to be introduced to show that the people were both numerous and well organized when they reached Kadesh, and therefore fully ready to enter the land if their eyes had been upon the Lord.

☐ **STUDY 2   Deuteronomy 2**

1   What do we learn from this chapter of the sovereignty of God over the nations? Cf. 32: 8; Acts 17: 26.

2   Why were Edom, Moab and Ammon spared on this occasion, whereas the Amorites were exterminated? Note verses 4, 5, 9, 19; and cf. Am. 1: 11 – 2: 3.

3   What do verses 24 and 31 teach about the relationship between divine grace and human faith? Cf. Eph. 2: 8.

Notes
1 Verse 1. 'Many days': nearly thirty-eight years; *cf.* verse 14.
2 Verses 4–8. This is not the same incident as that of Nu. 20: 14–21, but a later instruction when Israel had reached the eastern border of Edom.
3 Verses 10–12 and 20–23 are parenthetical notes on ancient history.
4 Verse 30. A judicial hardening, *i.e.*, to punish one already opposed to God.
5 Verse 34. 'Utterly destroyed': 'devoted to destruction', *i.e.*, under God's curse.

☐ **STUDY 3   Deuteronomy 3**

1 How did the conquest of Sihon and of Og disprove the faithless fears of forty years before? *Cf.* 1: 28 with 2: 36 and 3: 4–6. What use did later generations make of the memory of these victories? *Cf.* Jos. 2: 10; Pss. 135: 10, 11; 136: 18–20.

2 What do verses 21, 22 teach us about the duty of mutual encouragement? *Cf.* how Paul sought to share his assurance (2 Tim. 1: 12) with others (Phil. 1: 6).

3 Try to imagine the intensity of Moses' desire in verses 24, 25. What insight are we given into prayer and its answer by this incident? *Cf.* Nu. 20: 12; Ps. 106: 32, 33.

4 Verse 26: 'Let it suffice you.' Moses must be content with his own place in God's work. He was the law-giver, and Joshua (Hebrew form of 'Jesus') was the conqueror. How does Jn. 1: 17 throw light on this?

Notes
1 Verse 11. 'Bedstead': or possibly 'sarcophagus'. It was eleven feet long and six broad.
2 Verses 13–15. This double division of the tribe of Manasseh greatly weakened it, thus fulfilling Gn. 48: 14ff., in which Ephraim, although the younger of the two sons of Joseph, is given priority over Manasseh.
3 Verse 29. 'Beth-peor': 'house of Peor', the Moabite god through which the people sinned (Nu. 25).

☐ **STUDY 4   Deuteronomy 4: 1–40**

This is the second part of Moses' first discourse, and consists of an exhortation based upon God's gracious dealings, as described in chapters 1 to 3.

1 What is said about God in this portion, and about His relation to Israel?

2 What is said about the word of God, spoken by Moses? With verse 2 *cf.* 12: 32; Pr. 30: 6; Mt. 5: 17, 18; Rev. 22: 18, 19.

3 Against what sin in particular are the people warned, and by what arguments is the warning reinforced?

☐ **STUDY 5   Deuteronomy 4: 41 – 5: 33**

With chapter 5 begins Moses' second discourse, extending to chapter 26. Chapter 4: 44–49 is the introductory superscription.

1   What is the significance of the pronouns 'you' and 'your' which occur throughout the ten commandments? *Cf.* Lv. 19: 3; Ps. 62: 12; Je. 17: 10 ('every man').

2   The ways in which the people reacted to the hearing of the commandments (5: 23–27) indicate abiding principles concerning the ways in which all men should react to God's law. What kind of effect do the reactions here suggest that God's law should produce? *Cf.* Heb. 12: 21; Rom. 7: 9; Gal. 3: 24.

3   What was it in the temper of the people that drew from God the words of commendation in 5: 28, and the expression of His desire that it might so continue always (verse 29)?

Note .5: 3. 'Our fathers': *i.e.*, 'our forefathers', *viz.* the patriarchs. *Cf.* 4: 37; 7: 8.

☐ **STUDY 6   Deuteronomy 6**

In chapters 6–10 Moses outlines some *general* implications of the ten commandments before proceeding to apply them in detail to *particular* situations.

1   What was God's purpose in giving the law, and what was the primary duty of the Israelite? What was he to do, and what was he to beware of and not to do?

2   Verses 10–15 concern forgetfulness of God in a time of prosperity. What ways of guarding against this danger can be found either explicit or implicit in this passage?

3   What insight is given in this chapter into the necessity and method of family religion?

Notes
1   Verse 6. 'Be upon': literally 'imprinted on'.
2   Verse 13. Alluded to by Christ in answer to Satan (Mt. 4: 10).

☐ **STUDY 7   Deuteronomy 7**

1   In what *four* ways were the Israelites to deal with the idolatrous inhabitants of Canaan (verses 1–5)? What points regarding the Christian's duty of separation from sin and the world do they illustrate? *Cf.* Eph. 5: 11; 2 Cor. 6: 14–18; 1 Jn. 5: 21.

2   In verses 6–11 what *three* reasons does God give the people for this drastic attitude? What New Testament principles correspond to this? *Cf.* 1 Pet. 1: 15, 16; 2: 9–12.

3 In verses 12–16 what *three* blessings does God promise will attend the faithful pursuit of this policy? What blessings are promised in the New Testament to the Christian who practises spiritual separation? *Cf.* 2 Cor. 6: 17, 18; 1 Jn. 2: 15–17.

4 In verses 18–26 how does God answer their question of verse 17? What does this teach about the power given to the Christian to 'be separate'? *Cf.* 2 Cor. 2: 14–16; Jn. 16: 33; Rom. 5: 10; 1 Jn. 5: 4.

Notes
1 Verse 2. 'Utterly destroy': the Hebrew word means 'to separate to a deity' and hence 'to put to death' or 'destroy' as here, and in verses 25, 26.
2 Verse 20. 'Hornets' are powerful insects, whose attack in large numbers is dangerous and may prove fatal. Some take the word, however, here and in Ex. 23: 28 and Jos. 24: 12, in a figurative sense, as meaning some plague or terror that spreads dismay.

☐ STUDY 8 Deuteronomy 8

1 What threefold purpose did God have in leading Israel through the experiences of the wilderness? How did our Lord apply verse 3b to His own case in Mt. 4: 4? With verse 5 *cf.* also Heb. 12: 7, 10, 11.

2 In days of prosperity what subtle danger would beset them, and how were they to guard against it? Compare the advice which Barnabas gave to the church in Antioch (Acts 11: 23b).

☐ STUDY 9 Deuteronomy 9: 1 – 10: 11

1 After they conquered the promised land, what further danger would follow on the heels of victory? How does Moses in this passage seek to safeguard them against it? *Cf.* Lk. 18: 9–14.

2 What does the example of Moses teach as to the responsibility and power of intercessory prayer? Note the costly nature of his prayer and the uncompromising dealing with sin that accompanied it. On what grounds did Moses base his plea for the people, and what was the outcome? *Cf.* Jas. 5: 16.

3 The incident as a whole demonstrates that God's dealings with His people are entirely of grace. It thus illustrates aspects of the saving grace of God revealed in the New Testament. Try to discover how the following points are illustrated in this chapter: (a) the combination of grace and justice (Rom. 3: 24–26); (b) the triumph of grace over sin (Eph. 2: 5; Rom. 5: 20, 21); (c) the provision of a mediator (Heb. 8: 6; 9: 15); (d) the establishment of a covenant (1 Cor. 11: 25).

Note. 9: 22. 'Taberah': 'burning'; see Nu. 11: 1–3. 'Massah': 'proving'; see Ex. 17: 7; *cf.* Dt. 6: 16. 'Kibroth-hattaavah': 'graves of lust'; see Nu. 11: 34.

☐ **STUDY 10   Deuteronomy 10: 12 – 11: 32**

Moses here uses two main arguments to persuade the people to obedience:
(a) In 10: 12 – 11: 12 he shows that certain attributes and methods of God
demand a corresponding response from His people. (b) In 11: 13–32 he uses
the rewards of obedience and the punishments of disobedience as incentives.
This raises the following questions:

1   What specifically are the attributes and ways of God particular-
ized in 10: 12 – 11: 12 and what are their corresponding demands?

2   What rewards and punishments for obedience and disobedience
are specified in 11: 13–32?

Notes
1   10: 12. 'What . . . but . . .?' does not mean these demands are slight,
but that they are reasonable and to be expected in the light of God's character
and His calling of Israel to be His people. *Cf.* Mi. 6: 8.
2   11: 30. 'Moreh': where the Lord appeared to Abraham; see Gn. 12: 6, 7.

☐ **STUDY 11   Deuteronomy 12 and 13**

See Analysis. The first part of this code of laws sets forth regulations governing
the practice of religion, and is thus a detailed application of the first four
commandments.

1   How does chapter 12 relate to the first commandment and
chapter 13 to the second?

2   How do the regulations of chapter 13 demonstrate the priority
of God's will over alleged 'results', respect of persons, ties of blood
and great numbers? *Cf.* Mk. 13: 22; Gal. 1: 8; 2: 11; Lk. 14: 26;
Acts 4: 19, 20.

Note. The provision of one sanctuary to which all sacrifices must be brought
was a safeguard against idolatrous worship at ancient shrines of the Canaanites.
Cf. 2 Ki. 17: 10–12.

☐ **STUDY 12   Deuteronomy 14 and 15**

These two chapters contain laws concerning (a) funeral practices (14: 1, 2);
(b) clean and unclean foods (14: 3–21); (c) tithing (14: 22–29); (d) the seventh
year or year of release (15: 1–18); (e) firstling males of the herd or flock
(15: 19–23).

1   The principle underlying the laws of chapter 14 is that Christians
are to behave differently from the world. What do we learn here
concerning the Christian's attitude (a) to death and bereavement
(verses 1, 2; *cf.* 1 Thes. 4: 13); (b) to food and bodily indulgence
(verses 3–21; *cf.* 1 Cor. 6: 12, 13; 10: 23, 31); (c) to money and
possessions (verses 22–28; *cf.* 1 Cor. 16: 2)?

2   What do the laws of chapter 15 teach concerning (a) redemption
through Christ; (b) the Christian's duty of putting the need of his

brother before his own rights (*cf.* Mt. 5: 38–42); (c) equality in the church of God (*cf.* Acts 2: 44; 4: 34; 2 Cor. 8: 14)?

Notes
1 14: 1b. A reference to heathen mourning practices, signifying excessive grief.
2 15: 1. 'Grant a release': *i.e.*, let the debtor off.

□ **STUDY 13 Deuteronomy 16 and 17**

At 16: 18 the section on the civil law commences. Here we have (a) the appointment and duties of judges (16: 18–20); (b) justice in matters of religion (16: 21 – 17: 7); (c) the final court of appeal (17: 8–13); (d) the appointment and duties of the king (17: 14–20).

1 In connection with the Feast of Weeks and the Feast of Tabernacles, what two requirements are made of the worshipper, and why? With regard to free-will offerings, on what principle is the amount of the gift to be determined? *Cf.* 1 Cor. 16: 2; 2 Cor. 8: 12; 1 Pet. 1: 8.

2 What does 17: 2–7 teach us about the need for church discipline? *Cf.* Mt. 18: 15–18; 1 Cor. 5; 1 Tim. 1: 19, 20; Tit. 3: 9–11.

3 What was to be the character of Israel's king if one were appointed, and what was to be the source of his wisdom? *Cf.* 2 Tim. 3: 15–17.

Notes
1 16: 21. The Asherah appears to have been a pole, planted by an altar, as a symbol of the god worshipped there.
2 17: 8–13. If a case is too difficult for the local judge to handle (see 16: 18–20), it is to be brought to the central sanctuary.
3 17: 16, 17. Notice the word 'multiply' three times. Horses (power), wives, and wealth were coveted by kings of the time. *Cf.* 1 Ki. 10: 26–28; 11: 3, 4.

□ **STUDY 14 Deuteronomy 18 and 19**

In chapter 18 the offices of priest and prophet are included in the civil law since, Israel being a theocracy, these men were part of the government. Chapter 19 begins the section of laws governing social life, which are the detailed application of the last six commandments.

1 What were the special ministries of priests and prophets? Observe in chapter 18 how both alike were God's provision for His people's needs. Of what kind of person in heathen religion did the prophets in Israel take the place? How may we still distinguish between true and false prophets? *Cf.* Is. 8: 19, 20; 2 Pet. 1: 19; 2: 12.

2 In whom was the prophecy of 18: 18, 19 finally fulfilled? See Acts 3: 22, 23; 7: 37. Do we listen to Him as we should? *Cf.* Mk. 9: 7.

3   In what way do the regulations concerning cities of refuge both protect against injustice and at the same time enforce just penalty? See further Nu. 35.

4   How do the regulations of chapter 19 seek to apply the spirit as well as the letter of the sixth (verses 1–4), eighth (verse 14) and ninth (verses 15–21) commandments respectively?

Note. 19: 14. This law is intended to guard the inheritance of the poor against the greed of wealthy neighbours. *Cf.* 27: 17; Pr. 23: 10, 11.

□   **STUDY 15   Deuteronomy 20 and 21**

These laws relate indirectly to the sixth commandment and God's requirement of perfect justice in all walks of life.

1   What general principles may be deduced from chapter 20 regarding (a) the conduct of military warfare, and (b) spiritual warfare in the army of Christ? *Cf.* Lk. 14: 25–33.

2   What illustration do these chapters give both of the compassion and of the severity of God?

3   What application do the writers of the New Testament make of 21: 22, 23? *Cf.* Jn. 19: 31; Gal. 3: 13; 1 Pet. 2: 24.

□   **STUDY 16   Deuteronomy 22 and 23**

These laws are connected mainly with the sixth and seventh commandments.

1   22: 1–21. In what ways do these laws safeguard life, property and reputation, and thus put into operation the sixth commandment and the law of love to one's neighbour?

2   22: 13–30. How do these laws uphold the principle of chastity implicit in the seventh commandment? How do the laws and customs of our contemporary society compare?

3   23: 1–25. What steps were to be taken to maintain the purity of the congregation and thus of the worship of God? How is this applied in the New Testament to the church on earth and to heaven itself? *Cf.* 1 Cor. 5; Rev. 21: 27, and see Study 13.

Notes
1   22: 5. The distinction of the sexes, even in outward appearance, ought to be strictly maintained.
2   22: 9–11. Applied spiritually, these laws forbid the association of things morally incompatible; *cf.* 2 Cor. 14–16.
3   22: 14, 17. 'The tokens of virginity': *i.e.*, the sheet, which became stained with blood on the first coitus.
4   23: 15, 16. The reference appears to be a slave fleeing from a foreign country, and taking refuge in a city of Israel.

☐ STUDY 17 Deuteronomy 24 and 25

1 Chapter 24. The principle behind all these regulations is that of the eighth commandment: equity and honesty in all walks of life. Make a list of the ways in which this is to be practised according to this chapter. Examine your own life by these standards in order to discover points on which you are prone to fail.

2 What application does Paul make of 25: 4? See 1 Cor. 9: 9; 1 Tim. 5: 17, 18.

3 Taking Amalek as a type of 'the flesh', that is, of our fallen carnal nature, compare what is said here with Ex. 17: 14–16; Gal. 5: 17, 24. When and where is such an enemy most likely to attack, and how ought such an enemy to be regarded by us?

☐ STUDY 18 Deuteronomy 26

This chapter concludes both the social regulations and also the whole section of the specific laws to be observed by the people in the promised land.

1 Verses 1–11: *the law of first-fruits*, to be given to God, in acknowledgment of His mercies. In what way did the law require each Israelite to reflect upon and give thanks for national mercies, and for what mercies was he specially to give thanks? Have not we far greater cause to do this? *Cf.* Ps. 103: 1–5; Col. 1: 12–14.

2 Verses 12–16: *the law of tithes*, to be given to their ministers, and to others unable to provide for themselves. Note how richly God promises to give to those who thus give to Him and to others. *Cf.* 14: 28, 29; Pr. 3: 9, 10; Mal. 3: 8–12; Lk. 6: 38.

3 Verses 16–19 are the closing exhortation of the discourse begun in chapter 5. What covenant obligations did God and Israel respectively undertake? What may we learn from these verses concerning God's purposes for us as His covenant people?

☐ STUDY 19 Deuteronomy 27: 1 – 28: 14

See Analysis.

1 What ways does God use, through His servants, Moses, the elders and the priests, to impress upon His people how absolutely He requires obedience to all the laws of chapters 5–26?

2 What abiding principles emerge from chapter 27 concerning (a) the authority of ministers to pronounce judgment on sinners in God's name (*cf.* 1 Tim. 5: 20; Tit. 1: 13; 2: 15), and (b) the failure of the law to bring life? *E.g.*, although Israel literally obeyed verses

2–8 (see Jos. 8: 30–35), they soon broke the other laws. *Cf.* Rom. 8: 2–4; Gal. 3: 10–12.

3 Contrast the nature of the blessings of 28: 1–14 with the New Testament phrase 'every spiritual blessing in the heavenly places' (Eph. 1: 3). What difference between the old and new covenants is here indicated? To what extent do the promises of Dt. 28: 1–14 still apply to us?

Note. 27: 15–26. Note that the offences mentioned here are mainly such as might escape the detection and punishment of courts of law.

☐ **STUDY 20 Deuteronomy 28: 15–68**

Verses 15–19 are in direct contrast to verses 1–6. Thereafter the curses are described in five paragraphs, which are somewhat similar in content: (1) verses 20–26; (2) verses 27–37; (3) verses 38–44; (4) verses 45–57; (5) verses 58–68.

1 Examine these five paragraphs, noting their similarities. What are the evils contained in these curses?

2 This chapter shows God's people brought under a judgment worse than any that has befallen a heathen nation. It was fulfilled to some degree in the Assyrian and Babylonian captivities, but mainly in the Fall of Jerusalem in AD 70, and the subsequent history of the Jews. How does this emphasize the teaching that it is better not to begin to seek God rather than subsequently to turn away? *Cf.* Mt. 12: 43–45; Heb. 2: 1–4; 10: 26–31; 2 Pet. 2: 20–22.

Note. Verse 46. 'A sign and a wonder': a sign of divine judgment, and a wonder causing astonishment.

☐ **STUDY 21 Deuteronomy 29 and 30**

1 Picture the moving scene described in 29: 1, 2, 10, 11, and consider what strong reasons the people had for being loyal to the Lord. Why, then, did Moses fear that they would not prove steadfast? See 29: 4, 18, 19; *cf.* Acts 20: 29, 30.

2 For what purpose is revelation given, according to 29: 29? *Cf.* Jas. 1: 22. What is God's character as revealed in chapter 30? And what is His people's responsibility?

3 Compare 30: 11–14 with Rom. 10: 6–9 and note ways in which the Old Testament law and the New Testament gospel are identical.

Note. 29: 19. 'The sweeping away of moist and dry alike': a proverbial expression meaning 'to destroy *all*'. It expresses here that the outcome of the idolater's attitude and action is utter destruction.

☐ **STUDY 22   Deuteronomy 31**

1   What made it possible for Israel, and what makes it possible for us, to 'be strong and of good courage' and not to 'fear or be in dread' even when great human leaders pass away? See verses 1–8 and *cf.* Heb. 13: 7, 8.

2   In how many different ways did the Lord, through Moses, seek to safeguard Israel against the backsliding which He knew, never-theless, would take place? What alone can keep us steadfast? *Cf.* 1 Pet. 1: 5; Gal. 5: 16. *Cf.* also Dt. 32: 46, 47.

3   How does this chapter emphasize the need for something beside the law of God to promote obedience? *Cf.* Rom. 8: 3, 4; 2 Cor. 3: 5, 6.

☐ **STUDY 23   Deuteronomy 32: 1–47**

The analysis of this magnificent poem is as follows:
(a) The writer's purpose and hope, verses 1–3 (see Note 1 below).
(b) God's perfections, and Israel's perversity, verses 4–6.
(c) God's goodness to Israel, verses 7–14.
(d) Israel's backsliding, verses 15–18.
(e) Divine judgment upon Israel, verses 19–29.
(f) The victory of heathen nations over Israel is of God's permitting, verses 30–35.
(g) But He will finally avenge His people and show them His mercy, verses 36–43.

1   What is said of God in His essential attributes? And what, in contrast, of the nature of Israel?

2   What did God do for Israel (at least seven things are mentioned in verses 7–14), and how did Israel requite His loving-kindness?

3   What is God's purpose in His judgments, and what will be the final outcome?

Notes
1   Verse 2. 'May my teaching drop as the rain': an expression of the writer's hope that his words may act upon the hearts of men as the rain and dew upon the soil.
2   Verse 4. 'The Rock' (see also verses 15, 18, 30, 31, 37): a figure expressing the thought of a refuge and place of defence.
3   Verse 8. 'According to the number . . .': *i.e.*, He reserved for Israel an inheritance adequate to their numbers.
4   Verse 15. 'Jeshurun': a poetical name for Israel, signifying 'the upright one'. *Cf.* Dt. 33: 5, 26; Is. 44: 2.
5   Verse 29. 'Discern their latter end'; *i.e.*, discern whither their perversity must lead.
6   Verse 34. God is not unmindful of the sins of Israel's enemies.

☐ **STUDY 24   Deuteronomy 32: 48 – 34: 12**

Chapter 33, like Gn. 49, requires for its full understanding much research.

1   Chapter 33. Whence and why did these blessings come to the Israelites? Define for yourself the character or significance of each of the blessings here promised, and compare with them our blessings in Christ.

2   32: 48–52; 34: 1–12. Ponder (a) the character and work of Moses, and (b) the time and manner of his death. What may we learn from this record?

MARK   10 – 16

☐ **STUDY 20   Mark 10: 1–16**

1   Verses 1–12. What is Christ's teaching about divorce, and on what grounds does He base it?

2   Verses 13–16. No doubt the disciples were trying to be thoughtful here by guarding their Lord from unnecessary intrusion; why then was Christ so indignant? In what ways am I also in danger of obscuring Christ from those who are seeking Him?

3   Verse 15. What does it mean to 'receive the kingdom of God like a child', and why is this so essential? Cf. Mt. 18: 2–4.

☐ **STUDY 21   Mark 10: 17–31**

1   What basic wrong assumption was made by this man about salvation and eternal life? Cf. Eph. 2: 9. Why did Jesus stress to him the demands of the Law? What was the real hindrance that held him back?

2   Why did Jesus say it would be hard for those with riches to enter the kingdom? Cf. Lk. 14: 33. Are there any things in my life that are holding up spiritual progress?

3   What promises does Jesus make to those who are willing to renounce earthly wealth to follow Him without reservation? What is the meaning of the warning in verse 31? Cf. 1 Cor. 13: 3.

Note. Verse 25. 'There does not seem to be good early evidence for the view that the *eye of a needle* is a postern-gate in the city wall'. The phrase is better understood as a vivid description of sheer impossibility. (See *Mark* (TNTC), p. 165.)

□ **STUDY 22   Mark 10: 32–52**

1   Verses 32–34, 45. What new aspects of His sufferings does Jesus introduce here? Cf. 9: 31. Why does He continue to stress this subject? Why were His disciples amazed and afraid, and what ought we to be?

2   What motives do you think were behind the request of James and John, and what was the meaning of Christ's reply to them? Do our own aims in life also reveal the same spiritual shallowness? What is the governing principle of true Christian greatness?

3   What were the progressive steps which led Bartimaeus to the recovery of his sight? What can we learn from this incident that will both guide and encourage us when trying to help those who are spiritually blind to find their way to Christ?

Note. Verse 38. The terms 'baptism' and 'cup' are sometimes used symbolically in Scripture to denote suffering which has to be endured. In this passage they are forceful reminders of the cost of following Christ. Cf. Lk. 12: 50; Mk. 14: 36.

□ **STUDY 23   Mark 11: 1–19**

1   What truths concerning our Lord's Person are specially evident in the incidents here described? Jesus had previously refrained from publicly declaring His Messiahship. See 3: 11, 12; 8: 30; 9: 9. Why then did He declare it now?

2   Verses 1–6. When the two disciples were sent out by the Lord on this special errand, in what ways were they put to the test, and how would they benefit from the experience? Do we display the same faith and boldness in our service for Christ?

3   In what way does the fig tree described here typify Israel as a nation? What was Jesus seeking to teach His disciples from this acted parable? Before passing judgment, ought we not first to search our own hearts? Cf. Rom. 11: 20, 21.

Note. Verse 13. 'It was not the season for figs': it is fair to presume that the Lord was looking for the small early ripe figs that ripen with the leaves before the main crop.

☐ **STUDY 24   Mark 11: 20–33**

1   Verses 20–25. What does Jesus say here are the essential conditions of effective prayer? What more does prayer involve apart from just asking for pleasant things we desire? *Cf.* Mk. 14: 35, 36.

2   Why did Jesus refuse to answer the question put to Him by the Jewish leaders? What was the point of His question to them? Was He trying to be evasive? What was the root of the trouble, and how is this a warning to us? *Cf.* Heb. 3: 12.

Note. Verse 25. 'Unless we forgive our fellow men freely, it shows that we have no consciousness of the grace that we ourselves have received (Mt. 18: 32, 33), and thus that we are expecting to be heard on our own merits' (see *Mark* (*TNTC*), p. 181).

☐ **STUDY 25   Mark 12: 1–27**

1   Verses 1–12. How does this parable clarify Christ's unique position in relation both to God and to the prophets? What does it teach us (a) about the character of the motives which lay behind His final rejection, and (b) about His own expectation of vindication and victory?

2   Verses 13–17. How does this incident reveal both the wisdom of Christ and the insincerity of His questioners? What important truth was Jesus trying to convey to them, and of what relevance is this to us? *Cf.* Rom. 13: 1, 2, 6, 7.

3   Verses 18–27. The Sadducees were obviously attempting to make spiritual truth look ridiculous by interpreting it with the grossest of literalness. How does Christ show them their mistake? On what grounds does He base the certainty of the resurrection?

Note. Verses 1–12. Since the Lord was obviously using Isaiah 5: 1–7 as an Old Testament back-cloth for this parable, His hearers would know that He was referring to Israel, and that this was yet another parable of judgment. (See *Mark* (*TNTC*), pp. 183–184.)

☐ **STUDY 26   Mark 12: 28–44**

1   Verses 28–34. Jesus pronounced this scribe to be 'not far from the kingdom of God'. What would he have needed to do to enter in?

2   Verses 41–44. Jesus did not deny that the rich gave much, but merely stated that the widow had given more. What does this teach us about the way God measures our giving? How do we match up to this standard? *Cf.* 2 Cor. 8: 12; 9: 7.

3   The scribes undoubtedly had an intellectual mastery of Scripture and professed to accept its authority without question. Why then

did Christ condemn them and in what way is this a warning to us? *Cf.* Lk. 12: 47, 48.

☐ **STUDY 27   Mark 13: 1–23**

1   Verses 1–13. Notice how Christ translates the abstract enquiry of His disciples into the personal and moral realm. What spiritual dangers does He warn them about? How can we prepare ourselves to meet similar dangers?

2   Verses 14–23. What is here foretold? How are Christ's followers to act when it happens? To whom are they to look for deliverance? Of what are they to beware? What may we learn from such a passage concerning God's sovereignty and man's responsibility?

Notes
1   Verse 14. 'The desolating sacrilege': this is the sign of the impending destruction of the Temple for which the disciples had asked (verses 1–4). It refers to the desecration of the holy place by Roman invaders. *Cf.* Dn. 11:31.
2   Verse 15. 'Him who is on the housetop': the flat roofs of houses in Palestine were used for places of rest and social intercourse. *Cf.* Acts 10: 9.

☐ **STUDY 28   Mark 13: 24–37**

1   Among the many puzzling details of this passage concerning the coming of the Son of man, what are the facts about which we can be certain? What particular error do we need to avoid?

2   If we are expecting Christ to return, what difference should this make to the way we live our lives, and why? *Cf.* 2 Pet. 3: 10a, 11b, 14.

Notes
1   Verses 24, 25. The phraseology may, as in the Old Testament, symbolize national and international upheavals. *Cf.* Is. 13: 10; 34: 4; Ezk. 32: 7, *etc.*
2   Verses 33–37. 'Watch': *i.e.*, be wakeful and alert.

☐ **STUDY 29   Mark 14: 1–25**

1   Verses 1–9. What some said about the value of the ointment and the need of the poor was perfectly true. Why then did Jesus commend Mary for her extravagance? What does this incident teach us about right priorities in Christian service?

2   Verses 10–21. What do these verses suggest was the motive which lay behind Judas' act of betrayal? Is our own attitude one of condemnation, or are we prepared to share the solemn heart-searching of verse 19?

3   Verses 22–25. Consider the use here of the words 'bread', 'blood', 'my', 'gave', 'take', 'drank', 'covenant'. What light do they throw on the nature and method of salvation? *Cf.* 1 Pet. 1: 18, 19.

Notes

1 Verses 8, 9. Note Jesus' remarkable prediction of the future world-wide preaching of 'the gospel'; *cf.* 13: 10. There was in the woman's action a recognition both of the unique Person and of the impending work of Jesus; and these are both essential gospel truths.

2 Verse 22. The expression 'This is my body' corresponds to the Passover formula, 'This is the bread of affliction which our fathers ate in the land of affliction'. It indicates a symbolical commemoration, not an actual 'transubstantiation'.

☐ **STUDY 30   Mark 14: 26–52**

1 Verses 26–31. Peter evidently found it much easier to apply the Lord's words to the other disciples than to himself. What wrong attitude does this reveal? Do we ever refuse to accept what the Lord is plainly trying to teach us?

2 Verses 32–50. What caused our Lord's distress? What is meant here by 'the hour' and 'this cup'? Why was Jesus ready, in a way His disciples were not, for what had to be faced? What exactly was His petition? Was it answered. and if so, how? *Cf.* Heb. 5: 7, 8; Ps. 119: 50, 92.

☐ **STUDY 31   Mark 14: 53–72**

The object of the Jewish council was to find legal grounds for putting Jesus to death. It had been previously decided that He must die (14: 1), but some ground must be sought, which would justify their action in condemning Him, and enable them to secure Pilate's confirmation of the verdict. *Cf.* Lk. 23: 1, 2.

1 Verses 53–65. Note that the one definite charge, on which the decision to have Jesus put to death was taken, was His claim to be the Christ. *Cf.* 15: 26. How did Jesus declare that His claim would be vindicated? *Cf.* Acts 2: 32–36. What is your attitude to His claim?

2 Observe the experiences through which Peter passed on this eventful night. What were the contributing factors which finally led up to his denial of Christ? See 14: 29, 37, 50, 54. What can we learn from all this that will help us to be prepared for temptation?

☐ **STUDY 32   Mark 15: 1–21**

The main concern of the Jewish leaders now was to get their verdict carried into effect. For this they required the Roman governor's decision, for the Romans reserved to themselves the right of capital punishment.

1 What mistakes did Pilate make, and what were the reasons underlying them? Are there any of these that we are in danger of repeating? If so, what positive action can we take to avoid them?

2 Notice the amazing silence of Jesus (verses 4, 5; *cf.* 14: 60, 61a). Try, also, to picture the mocking of the soldiers, remembering that Jesus had just been scourged, a punishment of brutal severity. Why did Jesus submit without protest to such treatment, and why did God allow it to happen to Him? *Cf.* Phil. 2: 8; 1 Pet. 2: 22–24.

☐ **STUDY 33 Mark 15: 22–41**

1 With what words did the passers-by and the chief priests and scribes mock and revile Jesus? What have you seen, which they failed to see, which makes you believe that, nevertheless, He is the Christ?

2 What is the answer to the question in verse 34? What is the significance of the rending of the veil, and what consequent benefit can we now enjoy? *Cf.* Is. 59: 2; Gal. 3: 13; Heb. 9: 8; 10: 18–22.

☐ **STUDY 34 Mark 15: 42 – 16: 8**

1 What deliberate acts of Joseph are mentioned here? Considering who he was and the situation at the time, what qualities of character are shown by his behaviour? Which of these qualities is most lacking in my life?

2 Although the women who went to anoint the body of Christ were told that He had risen and they could see the empty tomb, and although they were given the privilege and the command to tell others, yet 'they said nothing to any one' (16: 8). Why was this? What did they still need to give them calmness, conviction and boldness in testimony? Are you at all like them?

☐ **STUDY 35 Mark 16: 9–20**

1 What three appearances of the risen Christ are recorded in these verses? What were the reasons for the rebuke of verse 14? Is our spiritual perception and growth hindered by the same two besetting sins? *Cf.* Heb. 3: 12, 13.

2 If we truly believe what is recorded in verse 19, what challenge and encouragement are there for us in verses 15 and 20? And what does verse 16 reveal concerning the issue with which the gospel confronts men, when it is preached? *Cf.* Rom. 10: 11–15.

Note. Verses 9–20. 'This section is the so-called "Longer Ending" of Mark, omitted in some MSS. . . . Therefore it seems reasonable to see this as an early attempt, known at least as early as Irenaeus, to "round off" a Gospel whose original ending had become in some way maimed or lost' (see *Mark* (*TNTC*), pp. 257–258).

JUDGES

Introduction

The author of the book of Judges is not known. The most likely date for the completion of the book is during the reign of David or the early part of Solomon's reign (observe the favourable attitude to the monarchy implied in 19: 1; 21: 25).

The book opens with an introductory section, in two parts. The first (1: 1 – 2: 5) gives extracts from a history of the conquest, stressing the failure of many of the tribes to possess their 'lots'. It also tells how they were rebuked by the angel of the Lord. The second (2: 6 – 3: 7) shows the falling away after Joshua's death and provides a summary of the salient features of the period. The main portion of the book (3: 8 – 16: 31) gives the history of the judges, of whom twelve are mentioned, namely, Othniel, Ehud, Shamgar, Deborah, Gideon, Tola, Jair, Jephthah, Ibzan, Elon, Abdon and Samson. It will be noted that the usurper Abimelech is not included. Six of the twelve judges (Othniel, Ehud, Deborah, Gideon, Jephthah and Samson) receive extended mention, whilst the other six are little more than named (for which reason they are sometimes referred to as 'the minor judges'). The final section of the book (17: 1 – 21: 25) narrates two instances of the moral and religious declension which characterized the period of the judges. The apostasy, lawlessness and immorality which they reveal are a vivid witness to a situation when 'every man did what was right in his own eyes' (17: 6; 21: 25).

The book bears testimony to the faithfulness of God, showing both His righteousness and His enduring mercy. It contains some memorable examples of faith, and reveals also the hideous blackness of human sin. There is also much instructive teaching in it on the workings of God's providence, especially in regard to the instruments which He can use in the working out of His purposes.

Analysis

I. The incomplete conquest (1: 1 – 2: 5).
- (a) 1: 1–21   The conquest of southern Canaan.
- (b) 1: 22–26   The capture of Bethel.
- (c) 1: 27–36   A catalogue of unoccupied territory.
- (d) 2: 1–5   The effect of the broken covenant.

II. Israel in the period of the judges (2: 6 – 16: 31).
- (a) 2: 6 – 3: 6   General introduction.
- (b) 3: 7–11   Othniel and Cushan-rishathaim of Aram.
- (c) 3: 12–30   Ehud and Eglon of Moab.
- (d) 3: 31   Shamgar and the Philistines.
- (e) 4: 1 – 5: 31   Deborah and Barak deliver Israel from Jabin and Sisera of Canaan.
- (f) 6: 1 – 8: 35   Gideon and the Midianites.
- (g) 9: 1–57   The usurper Abimelech.
- (h) 10: 1–5   Tola and Jair.
- (i) 10: 6 – 12: 7   Jephthah and the Ammonites.
- (j) 12: 8–15   Ibzan, Elon and Abdon.
- (k) 13: 1 – 16: 31   Samson and the Philistines.

III. Appendices
- (a) 17: 1 – 18: 31   Micah's household and the Danite migration.
- (b) 19: 1 – 21: 25   The outrage at Gibeah and the punishment of the Benjamites.

□ **STUDY 1 Judges 1: 1 – 2: 5**

The many parallels between this chapter and the book of Joshua show that it is a valuable supplementary account of the conquest. It deals with events *after* the main victories had been gained, when the tribes had dispersed to attempt the occupation of their allocated territory. The opening words of the book, 'After the death of Joshua', do not necessarily relate to the events of the first chapter, but are a general title to the complete book of Judges.

1 Judah began well. Why did they fail to complete their task? Ought their advance to have been checked by 'chariots of iron'? *Cf.* Dt. 20: 1; Jos. 17: 16–18; Jdg. 4: 13–15; Mt. 9: 29; Heb. 11: 33.

2 Notice the general movement from south to north in chapter 1. Can you document a corresponding deterioration in the situation as the chapter progresses?

3 What charge did the angel of the Lord bring against Israel? What were the consequences of their failure? What may we learn from this concerning the folly of compromise? *Cf.* Heb. 12: 14–17; Rom. 6: 16.

☐ **STUDY 2   Judges 2: 6 – 3: 6**

1   Backsliding, judgment, deliverance, renewed backsliding—trace this unvarying cycle in the history of the period, as summed up in this section. What sort of spiritual life corresponds to this in the life of the individual? *Cf.* Col. 3: 5, 6; Rev. 3: 1–3.

2   What may we learn from 2: 7, 10 and 3: 6 concerning the importance of (a) Christian example, (b) Christian teaching of the young, and (c) Christian marriage? *Cf.* Mt. 5: 13; Dt. 6: 6, 7; Eph. 6: 4; 1 Cor. 7: 39 (last clause); 2 Cor. 6: 14.

☐ **STUDY 3   Judges 3: 7–31**

1   Observe what the Lord did *against* Israel (verses 8 and 12), and what He did *for* Israel (verses 9 and 15). What caused Him to do the first, and what caused Him to do the second? What insight does this give into the principles of God's dealings with His people? *Cf.* Pss. 34: 12–18; 103: 8–14; 2 Ch. 7: 13, 14.

2   Compare and contrast Othniel and Ehud, both in their achievements and their methods. What quality was present in both men which enabled God to use them? *Cf.* 2 Ch. 16: 9.

☐ **STUDY 4   Judges 4**

1   Why do you think Barak was unwilling to undertake the campaign without Deborah? Does this reveal a defect in his faith? What insight does this give into God's willingness to bear with our human frailty? *Cf.* Ex. 4: 13–16; Je. 1: 6–8; 2 Cor. 3: 5, 6.

2   Who was the real architect of Israel's victory? *Cf.* Ex. 14: 13; 2 Sa. 8: 6, 14; 2 Ch. 20: 15–17. What practical application has this for us today?

☐ **STUDY 5   Judges 5**

The story falls into four parts: (a) verses 1–5, an introductory hymn of praise; (b) verses 6–8, the situation before the deliverance; (c) verses 9–18, the rallying of the tribes and the rebuke of the irresolute; (d) verses 19–31, the victory, and the death of Sisera.

1   Observe to what dire straits backsliding had reduced the tribes (verses 6–8; *cf.* 3: 31; 1 Sa. 13: 19, 22; 2 Ki. 10: 32, 33; 13: 3, 7). What parallel spiritual consequences are found in the life of the backsliding Christian?

2   What qualities are praised in the story, and what kind of conduct is condemned? Is there a present-day application in our service for God? *Cf.* Lk. 8: 14; 9: 62; Acts 15: 26.

Note. Deborah clearly approved of Jael's act, but did God approve? It was an act of treachery which abused all the accepted conventions of the age. It may be compared with Jacob's deceit of his aged father (Gn. 27), yet in both incidents there was an element which could be approved—Jacob's earnest desire for the blessing, and Jael's zeal for her people against their oppressor. In the case of Jacob we know that he suffered severely for his treachery, although he received the blessing.

☐ **STUDY 6   Judges 6**

The Midianite oppression took the form of an annual invasion (for seven years, 6: 1) of hordes of semi-nomads from Trans-Jordan. This is the first indication of the use of the camel in warfare (6: 5) which gave the Midianites an immense tactical superiority. The effect upon Israel is described in verses 2, 4 and 6.

1   When the people cried unto the Lord, what was His first answer? See verses 7–10, and *cf.* 2: 1, 2; Ps. 81: 8–11; Ho. 11: 1–4, 7.

2   Gideon was called to deliver Israel from the Midianites. But first he must make a stand for God in his own house (verses 25–32). Has this a bearing upon your Christian service? *Cf.* 2 Tim. 2: 19, 21; Mk. 5: 18, 19; Acts 1: 8.

3   By what three visible signs did God strengthen Gideon's faith? Consider what these signs would teach Gideon.

☐ **STUDY 7   Judges 7: 1–23**

1   What other principles, in addition to that expressly stated in 7: 2, appear in the choice of few out of many to be the instrument of God's victory? In answering, observe the character defects of those rejected in the two tests. *Cf.* 1 Cor. 9: 26, 27; 10: 12.

2   Consider the transformation in Gideon's attitude from spiritless acquiescence in bondage (6: 13, 15) to a complete assurance of victory (7: 15). Do you know such confident assurance in your battle against the forces of evil? *Cf.* Rom. 8: 37; 2 Cor. 2: 14; 1 Jn. 5: 4, 5.

☐ **STUDY 8   Judges 7: 24 – 8: 35**

1   Note (a) Gideon's dealings with the complaints of Ephraim and with the lack of co-operation of the elders of Succoth and Penuel; (b) the vigour of his pursuit and capture of Zebah and Zalmunna, and the respect which these princes showed him. What various aspects of character are here revealed?

2   What temptation did Gideon overcome? Contrast, however, the frequent references to God's guidance in the earlier part of the

narrative with the entire absence of this in 8: 24–27. Why did Gideon, who had given such able leadership in the national crisis, fail to give adequate leadership in a time of peace? Is it true that we tend to rely upon God only when we are 'up against it'?

Note. The ephod of the high priest (Ex. 28) was a shoulder garment covering the breast and back, ornamented with gems and gold, and having in front the breastplate containing the Urim and Thummim, which were manipulated to discover God's will. Gideon's ephod (8: 24–27) may have been an elaborate reproduction, or it may have been some kind of free-standing image. In any case it was used to ascertain God's answer in a particular situation, but the people came to regard it as a kind of idol.

□ **STUDY 9   Judges 9: 1 – 10: 5**

1   Consider in this story (a) the sin of Gideon in associating with a Shechemite woman and having a son by her (see 8: 31; *cf.* Dt. 7: 3); (b) the sin of the men of Shechem (9: 4, 5, 16–18); (c) the sin of Abimelech (9: 1–5). Compare verses 56 and 57 and consider how in each case the words of Nu. 32: 23b were fulfilled.

2   Shechem was a Canaanite city which, most probably, had been assimilated into Israel. What does this chapter teach us about the dangers of such a compromise?

Note. Verses 7–15. The first part of the parable contains a reference to 8: 22, 23. Verse 15 presents the incongruous picture of great trees seeking shelter under a lowly bramble, and being destroyed in a forest fire which originated in the very thorn bush whose shade they had sought. The point of the parable is not that the Shechemites had chosen a king, but that they had selected the wrong person to rule over them.

□ **STUDY 10   Judges 10: 6 – 11: 28**

1   Why did God, at first, refuse to deliver Israel from the Ammonites? What caused the change in His subsequent attitude? *Cf.* Je. 18: 5–11.

2   What indications are there in this section that Jephthah, in spite of his unfortunate background, possessed nobility, piety and faith?

3   Summarize Jephthah's answer to the Ammonites. To what extent do you find his arguments valid?

□ **STUDY 11   Judges 11: 29 – 12: 15**

1   Read the story of Jephthah's vow in the light of Ec. 5: 2–6; Dt. 23: 21–23. What does this story teach about (a) the sacredness of a promise to God, and (b) the necessity of first considering what such a promise may involve?

2 Compare Jephthah's treatment of the Ephraimites with that of Gideon in a similar situation (8: 1–3). What light does this incident throw upon (a) the Ephraimites, (b) Jephthah?

Note. Whilst all earlier commentators and historians accepted that Jephthah offered up his daughter in sacrifice, well-meaning scholars from the Middle Ages onwards have tried to reduce the maiden's fate to one of perpetual virginity. But the anguish of Jephthah (verse 35), the two-month reprieve (verses 37, 38) and the institution of an annual four-day feast would be inappropriate in such a situation. The plain statement of verse 39 must be allowed to stand.

☐ **STUDY 12   Judges 13**

1 How did Samson's Nazirite calling differ from that of the ordinary Nazirite vow? See Nu. 6: 1–5, 13–18.

2 Observe Manoah's concern (verses 8, 12) for guidance on the subject of the upbringing of the promised child. What lessons may present-day parents learn from this? *Cf.* Pr. 22: 6; 2 Tim. 1: 5; Heb. 12: 5–11.

3 What evidences of faith do you find in Manoah and his wife? And how did the wife's faith show itself to be greater than that of her husband?

☐ **STUDY 13   Judges 14 and 15**

1 Note the contradictory elements in Samson's character. He was a judge in Israel, yet his life-story centres around his dubious relationships with Philistine women. His unshorn locks denoted a Nazirite consecrated to God, yet his chief aim was to please himself. How many more such contrasts can you discover? How important is it that we should be consistent in our Christian profession? *Cf.* 2 Cor. 6: 14; 1 Thes. 5: 22.

2 What does the incident of 15: 18, 19 teach regarding God's ability to supply every need of His servants? *Cf.* 1 Ki. 17: 4, 9; Phil. 4: 19.

Note. The apathetic acceptance of the Philistine yoke by the men of Judah was the most dangerous feature of this period. Samson's one-man activity was used of God to bring the danger of complete Philistine domination out into the open.

☐ **STUDY 14   Judges 16**

1 What may we learn from this chapter concerning (a) the folly and fruit of sin; (b) the exultation of the ungodly at the downfall of God's servants; (c) God's enduring mercy to the penitent?

2   Contrast the sad end to Samson's life with its bright dawn in the sincere desire of his parents to rear him aright (13: 8, 12). Can you suggest reasons why Samson fulfilled so little of his potential? Under what conditions is it possible for the Christian to exhibit similar powerlessness?

☐ **STUDY 15   Judges 17 and 18**

The story of these chapters belongs to the later period of the judges, when Philistine pressure caused the complete displacement of the tribe of Dan and forced it to migrate northwards. There is therefore a general connection with the time of Samson. The tribal league was not functioning, and Micah had no court of appeal for the wrong done to him by the Danites. The narrative shows the decline of true religion and the lawless condition of the times.

1   How would you describe the religion of Micah and of the Danites? Wherein did they fall short of true religion?

2   A Levite was supposed to be a man who stood in a special relationship to God. What impression have you formed of this particular Levite? In what respects did he fail to walk worthily of his profession? Cf. Is. 61: 8a; Je. 23: 11; 1 Jn. 2: 4–6.

Notes
1   17: 7. 'Of the family of Judah': the words refer to the place Bethlehem, not to the Levite, who was only a 'sojourner' in Judah. There was another Bethehem in the land of Zebulun. Cf. Jos. 19: 15.
2   18: 30. 'The son of Gershom': the expression need only imply a descendant, not an actual father-son relationship.

☐ **STUDY 16   Judges 19**

Judges 19–21 belong to the period shortly after Joshua's death. Phinehas, the grandson of Aaron, was still alive (20: 28); there is no hint of foreign oppression; the league of tribes was still functioning.

1   What does this chapter teach us of the obligations of hospitality? Are there any indications of pitfalls to be avoided? Cf. Heb. 13: 1, 2.

2   There are many illustrations of evil in this chapter. Make a list of the chief sins shown here, and observe how the wickedness of the men of Gibeah brought destruction upon almost their whole tribe.

☐ **STUDY 17   Judges 20**

1   Gibeah was a Benjamite city, and the men of Benjamin refused to deliver up their fellow-tribesmen to justice. What is the relationship between loyalty to those with whom we are connected (family, friends, business associates, etc.) and our loyalty to God and His commandments?

2   Note the profound effect upon the tribes of the sin of the men

of Gibeah. See 19: 30; 20: 1, 8, 11. It stabbed the people awake to the degree to which moral declension had progressed among them. Can you discover other factors which show that *some* good came out of this sordid chapter of events?

3 How would you account for the fact that the eleven tribes were twice defeated by the Benjamites, even though they had asked counsel of the Lord? What do you gather from 20: 23 about their attitude? Was it a sign of weakness, or strength?

☐ **STUDY 18 Judges 21**

1 The tribes recognized after their victory that in the heat of the moment they had gone too far in making the vow of 21: 1. The sense of the unity of the tribes caused great distress at the thought that one tribe was in danger of extinction, in spite of the fact that they had suffered severely at the hands of Benjamin. How did they solve their dilemma? Did they keep, or break, their second vow (21: 5)? Would you condone the action they took in verses 10–12 and 19–23? What does the whole story suggest with regard to the taking of vows?

2 To what does the writer attribute this weak and unhappy condition of things in Israel? Do you consider this an adequate explanation of the moral and spiritual condition of Israel? If not, what would you add?

---

1 PETER

Introduction

This letter is attested by very early external evidence as a genuine writing of the apostle Peter. When Peter wrote it he was 'in Babylon' (5: 13). It seems best to regard this as a reference to Rome. A probable date for the writing of the letter is AD 63.

The letter is addressed to 'the exiles of the dispersion' in Asia

Minor. But though Peter was the apostle of the circumcision, and the term 'dispersion' was ordinarily applied to the Jews scattered among the nations, the letter itself contains clear evidence that its readers at least included converted Gentiles (1: 14; 2: 9, 10; 4: 3, 4), who were addressed as the spiritual Israel dispersed among the heathen.

The letter had a double purpose: to comfort and encourage the Christians in a time of persecution actual or threatened; and to exhort them, all the more on account of this danger, to holiness of living and to hope of glory. The problem of suffering, especially the suffering of God's people, was the main subject of the book of Job, and we have met with contributions to its solution in Isaiah and in the Gospel of John. In this letter, as in Job, it is of primary importance, and here we find a noble and satisfying answer to Job's despairing questionings. Compare, for example, Jb. 10 with 1 Pet. 1: 6–9. Peter has a key to the problem which Job had not. He knew that a sinless One had suffered and died, bearing our sins in His body on the tree; so that undeserved suffering has the halo of His glory round it, and to bear it aright is to follow in the steps of the Redeemer. Also, His resurrection and heavenly enthronement (1: 21; 3: 22) are proof that suffering in the will of God leads to certain eternal reward.

Analysis

☐ **STUDY 1   1 Peter 1: 1–12**

1   What do Christians mean by 'salvation'? How is it provided? What benefits does it offer? What kind of understanding and response are essential to its full enjoyment?

2   How can Christians 'rejoice with unutterable and exalted joy' while they 'may have to suffer various trials' (verses 6, 8)? What causes of joy does Peter enumerate in verses 3–9?

3   What light is thrown in verses 10–12 upon (a) the work of the prophets, (b) the ministry of the Spirit, and (c) the task of preachers of the gospel? What is their common interest and concern? Is it yours?

Note. Verse 2. 'Sprinkling with his blood': this signifies, for all who come under it, the ratification of the new covenant, and personal participation in its blessings and demands. *Cf.* Ex. 24: 7, 8; Heb. 9: 19–22; 12: 24; 13: 20, 21.

☐ **STUDY 2   1 Peter 1: 13 – 2: 3**

1   What has God provided to make possible (a) our redemption, (b) our new birth, and (c) our growth to full salvation? What response is necessary on our part to enjoy the benefits divinely intended for us?

2   In what ways ought our new God-given life as Christians to be expressed? What changes or new standards should characterize our daily living?

Notes
1   1: 17. 'With fear': *i.e.*, 'with reverence and awe'. *Cf.* Heb. 12: 28.
2   1: 17. 'Your exile': *i.e.*, your temporary sojourning in a place to which you no longer belong. *Cf.* 2: 11.
3   1: 19. 'Blood' here signifies blood shed, or life laid down, in sacrificial death.
4   2: 2. 'Spiritual milk': in Greek the adjective is *logikos*. 'Logical' milk suggests food for the mind rather than the stomach. Mention in 1: 23 of the divine 'logos' or 'word' suggests a further reference here to the same divine agent, the 'milk of the word' (AV).

☐ **STUDY 3   1 Peter 2: 4–17**

1   Verses 4–10. Under what figures does Peter here speak of the Christian church? What determines whether men find a place in it or not? Each figure suggests special blessings and responsibilities. Seek to identify these, and to face up to the practical challenge of each.

2   Verses 11–17. What instructions concerning worthy Christian conduct are given here? In what ways are a right attitude and

corresponding right action important (a) for our own spiritual well-being, and (b) for effective witness for God in the world? How can God use our 'good conduct'? *Cf.* Mt. 5: 16.

Notes
1 Verses 4–8. Peter justifies his comparison of Christ to a stone from three Old Testament passages: Ps. 118: 22; Is. 8: 14; 28: 16. To the believer Christ is the corner-stone on which the whole building depends; to the unbeliever He is a cause of stumbling.
2 Verse 16. 'A pretext for evil': *i.e.*, 'an excuse for base conduct' (Weymouth). *Cf.* Gal. 5: 13.

☐ **STUDY 4   1 Peter 2: 18–25**

1   In what ways does Christ's suffering provide an example for us to follow? What does Peter here suggest that 'servants' or 'slaves' should learn from it? Do I need to appreciate that this is also part of my Christian calling?

2   Why was the sinless Jesus willing without protest to submit to the full penalty due to the worst of sinners? What purpose was His sacrifice intended to serve? What response and what results ought to follow in my life?

Note. Verse 24. 'Bore our sins': to 'bear sin' means to 'endure its penalty'. 'On the tree': the wording suggests 'up on to the tree', *i.e.*, to the extreme limit of shameful crucifixion and, in Jewish eyes, of coming openly under the curse of heaven. *Cf.* Dt. 21: 23; Gal. 3: 13.

☐ **STUDY 5   1 Peter 3: 1–12**

1   Verses 1–7. What qualities in wife and husband make for a happy and harmonious wedded life? In addition, what special results can sometimes follow if the individuals concerned behave as a Christian wife or husband should?

2   Verses 8–12. What characteristics are mentioned here which should mark Christians in their relations (a) with one another, and (b) with non-Christians who work or speak evil against them? What is the way to blessing according to (a) Ps. 34: 12–16 (here quoted), and (b) our Christian calling? *Cf.* Mt. 5: 11, 12, 44, 45. Apply these standards to your own life in self-examination and prayerful concern.

☐ **STUDY 6   1 Peter 3: 13 – 4: 6**

1   3: 13–17. In what spirit should the Christian (a) face suffering 'for righteousness' sake', and (b) explain his faith and hope to a hostile questioner?

2 3: 18 – 4: 3. What were the nature, purpose and issue of Christ's sufferings? How, in consequence, ought we to face, and to spend, the rest of our earthly lives?

Notes

1 3: 14. Such suffering should be regarded not as one's unhappy lot, but as an added privilege. *Cf.* 4: 13, 14. It means one is the object of special divine favour. *Cf.* Lk. 1: 48. If God so wills it (3: 17), such suffering must be for some good reason and purpose. See 3: 18; 4: 1.

2 3: 18b–20. After His death on the cross Christ was at once able, as One alive in the spirit, to go and proclaim His triumph to the rebellious and imprisoned evil spirits who had involved men in sin and judgment.

3 3: 20. In the ark Noah and his family were 'saved through water', *i.e.*, brought safely through the judgment of God which fell upon a sinful world.

4 4: 6. This is best understood as meaning that this is why the gospel was preached during their earthly lives to those believers who are now dead.

☐ **STUDY 7   1 Peter 4: 7–19**

1 Verses 7–11. In what practical activities ought all Christians to engage? Make a brief list of them from this passage. In what way do they all start? At what end should they all aim? What is my gift (verse 10), and am I properly exercising it in ministry?

2 Verses 12–19. What kinds of suffering should the Christian (a) avoid, and (b) rejoice in? How should the latter kind of suffering be faced, and what good may be expected to issue from enduring it?

Note. Verse 14b: *i.e.,* because God will specially manifest His presence to you and with you. *Cf.* Ex. 40: 34.

☐ **STUDY 8   1 Peter 5**

1 Verses 1–4. How is oversight or the shepherd-care of God's flock to be exercised? What characteristics should a good pastor (a) avoid, and (b) exhibit? Note (a) how Peter speaks of himself, and (b) who is the chief Shepherd.

2 Verses 5–14. What according to these verses is 'the true grace of God', and how are we to 'stand fast in it' (verse 12)? In other words, what purpose is God working out for our good, and what must we do to co-operate with Him, and to enjoy the full enrichment of all His grace?

RUTH

Introduction

The general tone shows the setting of the story to be that of the time of the Judges. The book was read at the time of the Feast of Pentecost. The outstanding lesson of the book is the way in which the hand of God is seen guiding the faithful in the details of everyday life, as also in the events through which the way was prepared for the birth of the Son of David (see Mt. 1: 5).

Analysis

1: 1–22   Ruth's faithfulness to Naomi.
2: 1 – 4: 12   Ruth's contact with Boaz.
4: 13–22   Ruth's marriage.

☐ **STUDY 1   Ruth 1 and 2**

1   Put yourself in Ruth's place, and consider the cost of her decision to follow Naomi into the land of Israel. Orpah, too, had been a good daughter (1: 8), but what differences were there between her attitude and Ruth's? What lessons may Ruth teach us about our following Christ? Cf. Lk. 9: 23, 57–62; 14: 25–33.

2   Notice how an apparently chance happening (2: 3, 20) was overruled by God for blessing. Can you recall similar experiences? Also, in chapter 2 what qualities are outstanding (a) in Boaz, and (b) in Ruth?

Note. For the background to chapter 2 see Lv. 23: 22.

☐ **STUDY 2   Ruth 3 and 4**

1   How does the whole story show the Lord's loving-kindness to those who trust Him? Cf. La. 3: 22–26, 31–33; Na. 1: 7; Rom. 8: 28.

2   What example are we given in chapter 4 on matters affecting the rights of others?

Note. 3: 12. 'Near kinsman': the Hebrew word (*goel*, meaning 'next of kin') has a technical meaning in Hebrew law. The next of kin had certain duties and privileges, among them being that of redeeming the land or person of a kinsman who had been compelled to sell his land or himself through poverty (*cf.* Lv. 25: 25, 47–49). To draw a portion of a kinsman's mantle over oneself (3: 9) was the legal way of claiming protection and redemption. A kinsman-redeemer must be able and willing to redeem and pay the redemption price in full. *Cf.* 4: 4–6; Gal. 3: 13, 14.

---

1 SAMUEL

Introduction

The two books of Samuel formed a single work known as 'Samuel' in the Hebrew Canon. The Septuagint translators made the division. They grouped 1 and 2 Samuel with the two books of Kings to form the four 'Books of the Kingdoms'. The story is that of the development of the nation from the state described at the end of Judges to the established monarchy under David and the events of David's reign.

The chief religious theme is that Israel are the people of God, who alone is their true Ruler. First, they are rebuked for their decadence and sin by Samuel, who accedes to their demands for a king. But he warns them fully of the consequences. Saul, the sort of king the people wanted, is anointed at God's command and his history proves the danger to the nation of a self-willed leader. Finally, David is appointed and leads the people with the one aim of pursuing the will of God, until in his turn he falls into sin. The incidental events are all evidences of the inherent sinfulness of the natural man and proof of the enabling power of God granted to those who go forward in faith, as Samuel and David did. The underlying history is a continuation of that of the Pentateuch and Judges, with the theme 'a people for my name'.

Analysis

1 – 6   Eli's high-priesthood and its failure.
7 – 15   Samuel as judge; the first king rejected.
16 – 31 David during the reign of Saul.

☐ **STUDY 1   1 Samuel 1**

1   Verses 1–16. List the phrases describing Hannah's distress. Do you find her retaliating against her rival? How did she dispel her grief? *Cf.* Pss. 62: 8; 142: 1–3; 1 Pet. 2: 23.

2   Account for the change of verse 18b. How can a similar experience be mine? *Cf.* Mk. 11: 24; Jn. 4: 50; 1 Jn. 5: 15.

3   With verses 26–28 compare Ps. 116: 12–14; Ec. 5: 4, 5. Do you find all the encouragement you ought in the faithfulness and unforgetfulness of the Lord?

☐ **STUDY 2   1 Samuel 2: 1–11**

This Old Testament 'Magnificat' (*cf.* Lk. 1: 46–55) possesses an astonishing range of ideas concerning the character of God, His dealings with all sorts of men even to the ends of the earth, and the coming of His anointed king.

1   Compare the exaltation of verse 1 with the dejection of 1: 6–10. What or who should be the object of our joy? *Cf.* Pss. 9: 1, 2; 5: 11, 12; 1 Pet. 1: 8.

2   What does Hannah say about (a) God's character, and (b) the way in which time and again He reverses the lot of men? What will be the final end as described in verses 9, 10? What warning and what encouragement do you take from these truths? *Cf.* Ps. 2: 11, 12.

Note. Verse 6. 'Sheol' was the Hebrew name for the place where the dead go.

☐ **STUDY 3   1 Samuel 2: 12–36. (Read also 3: 11–14)**

1   What aspects of the sins of Eli's sons were specially grievous in God's sight? See 2: 12, 17, 25, 29; 3: 13. What serious warning ought we to take from 2: 25, 30 and 3: 14?

2   How did Eli fail? *Cf.* Pr. 29: 17; Mt. 10: 37. Over against 2: 31 and 3: 14 set 2: 35. What may we learn from all this concerning the ways of God? *Cf.* 16: 1.

Notes
1   Verses 12–17. The misappropriation of Eli's sons ('the men' of verse 17) was twofold. They took what they wanted rather than what was offered them; and they insisted on receiving their raw portion, before the Lord's portion—the fat (Lv. 3: 3–5)—was burned upon the altar.

2 Verses 18, 28. The 'ephod' was an item of priestly dress or equipment.
3 Verse 25. The tense shows that Eli's sons habitually did not listen to their father. Notice that it was the Lord's will to slay them for disobedience, but not the Lord's will that they should be disobedient.
4 Verse 30. 'Go in and out before me': a phrase describing the enjoyment of God's favour. Cf. verse 35.

☐ STUDY 4 1 Samuel 3: 1 – 4: 1a

1 Notice the expressions used about Samuel in 2: 18, 21; 3: 1, 7, 19. What new thing came into Samuel's life in the experience described in 3: 1–14? Why did Samuel have to tell the vision (3: 15–18)? Cf. 1 Cor. 9: 16.

2 What was lacking in Israel at this time, and what did God do to meet the need? Do you know places that need similar divine provision? Cf. Jn. 1: 6, 7; Lk. 3: 2, 3; Rom. 10: 14, 15.

Notes
1 3: 1. In those days there was no prophet regularly active to give the people messages from God; contrast 3: 20 – 4: 1a.
2 3: 10. 'The Lord . . . stood forth': this vivid language is paralleled in Jb. 4: 15, 16.

☐ STUDY 5 1 Samuel 4: 1b–22

1 Try to picture what a crushing blow these events were for Israel. What is the right answer to the question 'Why?' in verse 3?

2 The ark was the visible symbol of the Lord's 'glory' or manifested presence (see verses 21, 22). Why, then, did the Israelites' use of it prove unavailing? In what ways may Christians today make a similar mistake?

☐ STUDY 6 1 Samuel 5: 1 – 7: 2

1 Read the story of 5: 1–5 in the light of Je. 10: 1–16. Contrast the idols with the Lord of hosts. How ought such evidence to influence our fears and our faith?

2 Because the ark of the Lord was associated with His law (cf. Dt. 31: 9), it was also associated with judgment—as in this passage. Why did such a dire punishment fall on the men of Beth-shemesh, and with what result? Cf. Ex. 19: 21; Heb. 12: 28, 29; and see Note 2 below.

Notes
1 5: 6, 12; 6: 4, 5. The association of tumours and mice suggests an outbreak of bubonic plague.
2 6: 19. The ark, according to God's command, was to be kept closely covered, when not in the Holy of Holies. Cf. Nu. 4: 5, 6, 15, 20.

☐ STUDY 7   1 Samuel 7: 3 – 8: 22

1   How does the story of chapter 7 reveal the conditions of victory even on the field of former defeats? Have you had some such experience?

2   Wanting a king was not necessarily wrong (*cf.* Dt. 17: 14, 15), especially in view of the situation described in 8: 1–3. Why then did God, while granting their request, at the same time rebuke the people for making it? Why was the desire to be 'like all the nations' (8: 5, 10) wrong? Contrast Samuel's actions with the attitude of the people.

Notes
1   7: 6. The pouring out of water symbolized separation from sin.
2   8: 7. The 'you' and 'me' in the last clauses are emphatic. The people were rejecting God (*cf.* 10: 19), as later Saul did (15: 23).
3   8: 10–18. The behaviour described is typical of oriental despots.

☐ STUDY 8   1 Samuel 9: 1 – 10: 16

This passage describes Saul's private anointing to be king. 10: 20–24 describes his public identification by lot as the man of God's choice. 11: 14, 15 describes his public enthronement.

1   9: 1–14. What encouragement may we take from the fact that the free movements of young men and girls, of asses and God's prophet, are here overruled to bring about God's purposes?

2   What three confirmatory signs were given to Saul? How would they give him assurance that Samuel's words in 10: 1 were indeed true? How does this section also show that when God calls, He equips?

Notes
1   10: 3, 4. It was remarkable that the men should give Saul part of the offering which they probably intended to sacrifice at the sanctuary.
2   10: 8. *Cf.* 13: 8–14. The event of 11: 14, 15 is an interlude and not the visit to Gilgal referred to in 10: 8.

☐ STUDY 9   1 Samuel 10: 17 – 11: 15

1   How does the story of Saul's public election demonstrate God's forbearance? See especially 10: 19. *Cf.* Pss. 103: 14, 15; 78: 37–39; Rom. 2: 4.

2   To what does Scripture attribute Saul's vigorous action and his success? *Cf.* Acts 1: 8. Do these verses come to you as a challenge, or a rebuke?

3   Consider what noble qualities Saul displays. See 9: 21; 10: 9, 16b, 22, 27c. Does your life give evidence of a similar work of God?

Note. 11: 9. The men of Jabesh never forgot Saul's rescue of them from the Ammonites. See 31: 11–13.

☐ STUDY 10 1 Samuel 12

1 What was the point of Samuel's historical recital? Unlike the Israelites, do we (a) remind ourselves constantly of the great things God has done for us, and (b) allow this reminder to have a full effect upon our behaviour?

2 What were the outstanding features in Samuel's character as seen in this chapter?

3 Summarize the counsels and warnings of verses 20–25. Note especially what Samuel says about prayer. Yet, if the people will not turn from their wicked ways, will prayer avail? See verse 25; *cf.* Je. 15: 1; Ps. 99: 6, 8.

☐ STUDY 11 1 Samuel 13

1 Consider the Israelites' great danger. See verses 5, 6, 19–22. In such a situation what ought they to have known to be the one indispensable and sure secret of survival and victory? See 12: 14, 15.

2 What was wrong with Saul's professed desire to entreat the favour of the Lord, and with the action he took to further it? What warning do you take from the irreparable consequences following on one specific sinful act? Why does God expose men to such searching tests? See Dt. 8: 2.

Notes
1 Verse 1. Some numbers are lacking here. Thirty would in each case suitably fill the gap.
2 Verse 2. Many years must have elapsed. In 9: 2 Saul is described as a 'young man'. Here his son Jonathan is old enough to command a fighting force.

☐ STUDY 12 1 Samuel 14

1 How was it that Jonathan was so courageous? *Cf.* verse 6 with 2 Ch. 14: 11; 1 Sa. 2: 9, 10.

2 What indications do you find of Saul's impatience, and how did it lead him to hasty and wrong decisions? Yet what evidence is there that with all his self-will Saul was anxious not to offend the Lord? How do you account for this?

Notes
1 Verse 6. 'The Lord will work for us': the Old Testament is full of the God who *acts* in different ways. *Cf.* 1 Ki. 8: 32; Je. 14: 7; Ps. 22: 30, 31.
2 Verse 24. Saul's purpose was probably religious, *viz.*, by fasting to obtain God's favour.

☐ **STUDY 13   1 Samuel 15**

1   Trace the course of Saul's disobedience—his excuses (verses 20, 21, 24) and his self-interest (verse 30). Trace also the course of Samuel's warning (verse 1), denunciation (verses 14, 18, 19), and declaration of divine judgment (verses 22, 23, 26, 28, 29). What may we here learn concerning God's ways and the demands of His service?

2   From verse 11, and from Samuel's reply to Saul in verses 22, 23, what do we learn concerning the divine reaction against ritual without obedience, against outward religious observance which masks an inner disobedience? Have God's requirements or His attitude changed?

Notes
1   Verse 15. The whole point about the sacred ban was that *everything* must be destroyed; not one thing must be spared or looted. Cf. Jos. 7: 1.
2   Verse 35. 'Samuel did not see Saul again.' 'See' here means 'visit' or 'go to see'. So 19: 24 involves no contradiction with this passage.

☐ **STUDY 14   1 Samuel 16**

1   How is true obedience illustrated in Samuel's behaviour? What can you learn from his example?

2   What great truth was brought home to Samuel at Bethlehem? Consider how this truth is emphasized in Jesus' teaching. See Mt. 6: 1; 7: 15, *etc.* Cf. Rom. 2: 28, 29.

3   Here men twice sent to fetch David; why? When he comes into sight, what do we learn about him? Make a list of his characteristics. What was the chief evidence that God had chosen him and rejected Saul? Cf. 2 Cor. 1: 22.

Note. Verses 21, 22. David became an 'armour-bearer'—possibly a military title. The phrase 'remain in my service' does not imply continued physical presence. If it did, 17: 55, 56 would be unintelligible.

☐ **STUDY 15   1 Samuel 17: 1–54**

1   What was it that made David view the situation differently, and gave him courage, when all the men of Israel were much afraid? Cf. Ps. 42: 5, 11; Is. 51: 12, 13.

2   How did David's past experiences of the Lord's deliverance give him confidence to face the present challenge? What practical lessons does this teach about (a) the value of remembering, and (b) the importance of proving God's presence and power in ordinary daily living?

3 What do you think of Saul's reasoning (verse 33), and of his provision for David (verses 38, 39)? Did he understand what he was saying, in his words to David: 'The Lord be with you!'? What was lacking? See verse 47.

Notes
1 Verses 4ff. The giant was over nine feet tall, and carried 125 lb. of armour.
2 Verse 18. 'Some token': *i.e.*, that they are well, *etc.*

☐ **STUDY 16 1 Samuel 17: 55 – 19: 24**

1 How were fear and jealousy like a cancer in Saul's spirit? How did they show themselves? How do you explain God's action in this matter? By what means were Saul's attempts to destroy David foiled?

2 How did Jonathan and Michal show their love for David? Do we ever risk anything for our friends? See 1 Jn. 3: 16, 18.

Notes
1 18: 5. 'Was successful': a pregnant Hebrew word is used meaning 'deal wisely' with the implied consequence of success. *Cf.* Is. 52: 13a.
2 18: 10. *Cf.* 1 Ki. 22: 22.
3 19: 13. 'An image': Hebrew 'teraphim', *i.e.*, household gods; *cf.* Gn. 31: 19. This deceived Saul's messengers into thinking that David was ill in bed.
4 19: 23, 24. 'Naked': *i.e.*, with his outer garment laid aside; *cf.* Is. 20: 2; Mi. 1: 8. Saul lay in a trance for a day and a night. The origin of the proverb about Saul is recorded in 10: 12. His behaviour here evidently caused men to recollect it.

☐ **STUDY 17 1 Samuel 20: 1 – 21: 9**

1 What was David's purpose in seeking Jonathan? What request did Jonathan in turn make of David? What components of true friendship does the relationship of these two men illustrate?

2 What characteristic of true 'loyal love' (20: 14) does this passage reveal? Compare it with (a) 1 Cor. 13: 4–7, and (b) your own life.

3 When human need and ceremonial obligations conflict as in 21: 6, what guidance do we find here as to the right course to take? *Cf.* Mt. 12: 3–8.

Notes
1 20: 6. Such were the standards of morality that even the best of the people seemed to have no scruples in using lies and deception to save life. See 19: 17; 20: 28, 29; 21: 2. But note how deceit brought down Saul's wrath upon Jonathan (20: 30), just as it brought disaster upon Ahimelech and his associates (22: 18, 19).
2 20: 14. *Cf.* 2 Sa. 9: 3.

3   20: 23, 42. The idea of God being between two covenant partners to watch and to judge is illustrated by Gn. 31: 49, 53.

4   20: 26. Saul thought that ceremonial uncleanness accounted for David's absence from the feast. See Lv. 7: 19, 20.

5   21: 7. 'Detained before the Lord': perhaps because of a vow.

STUDY 18   1 Samuel 21: 10 – 22: 23

1   Do you gather from 21: 10–15 and 22: 3–5 that David's flights out of the holy land were done without God's guidance? What seems to have determined David's actions? Contrast 22: 23. Are you free from the fear of men? *Cf.* Pr. 29: 25.

2   Consider the character of the motley crew of which David now became the leader. Why did they turn to him? How can God today transform any group under Christian leadership? *Cf.* 1 Cor. 6: 9–11; note especially the phrase, 'such were some of you'.

3   Read the story of 22: 7–19 in the light of Pr. 6: 34; 14: 30; 27: 4. How can the Christian be zealous without being jealous? *Cf.* 1 Ki. 19: 10, 14; Jn. 2: 17.

STUDY 19   1 Samuel 23 and 24

1   In what ways did God's protecting hand cover David, and what special encouragements did he receive? *Cf.* Ps. 37: 23, 24.

2   What held David back from killing Saul when it was in his power to do it, and when his followers were urging him on? What virtues shine out in his self-restraint, and what lessons do you learn from this? *Cf.* Rom. 12: 19, 20.

3   Were Saul's words and weeping accompanied by a real change of heart? *Cf.* Ho. 6: 4; Is. 29: 13. What does real repentance involve?

Notes

1   24: 13, 14. David uses the proverb to demonstrate his innocence. The wicked action one would expect from a wicked man has not been forthcoming in his case. 'A dead dog . . . a flea': something harmless, elusive, unimportant.

2   24: 20, 21. Saul apparently knew God's purpose, though he strove to avert some of its consequences.

STUDY 20   1 Samuel 25 and 26

1   Nabal was rich and satisfied; but what did he lack? What, in contrast, were the outstanding features of Abigail's character? Can you think of situations where you could act as she did?

2 Chapter 26. What basic convictions motivated David's actions? How does his faith in God's purpose for him stand out? In particular, what principle emerges from 25: 39 and 26: 10, 23?

Note. 26: 19, 20. To be driven out of the promised land (*cf.* 27: 1) is to be driven out not from the dominion of the Lord (see many psalms), but certainly from His special covenanted presence to lands where other gods are worshipped.

☐ **STUDY 21   1 Samuel 27 and 28**

1 Contrast David's words in 27: 1 with 17: 37. Into what action did depression drive him, and what price had he to pay for it? Are you ever overcome by circumstances in this way? *Cf.* 2 Ch. 19: 2; Jas. 4: 4.

2 Looking back over the story of Saul, how did he come to his final sorry state? What warning ought we to take from his confession in 28: 15? *Cf.* 1 Tim. 1: 19.

Note. 28: 7. Consulting a medium was expressly forbidden in the law of God. See Lv. 19: 31. Saul, too, was resorting to something he himself had disowned. See 28: 9.

☐ **STUDY 22   1 Samuel 29 and 30**

1 Chapter 29. Into what great difficulty had David brought himself, and how was he delivered? Do I ever give the world cause to say, 'What is that Christian doing here?' *Cf.* 2 Cor. 6: 14.

2 Chapter 30. Strength in defeat and generosity in victory. How does this chapter illustrate these characteristics? Have you learnt David's secret of inner strength? *Cf.* 23: 16; Ps. 18: 2.

☐ **STUDY 23   1 Samuel 31 and Revision**

1 Compare the defeat of chapter 31 with that of chapter 4. What were the reasons for these defeats? *Cf.* 1 Ch. 10: 13, 14. What challenge does this bring to your own life?

2 How did David's experiences, as recorded in chapters 16–31, all serve to prepare him for his future work as king?

EPHESIANS

Introduction

This Epistle, together with Philippians, Colossians and Philemon, form a group known as the 'Prison' Epistles, because all four were, as is generally believed, written from Rome when Paul was a prisoner there, as described in Acts 28: 16, 30, 31. The words 'at Ephesus' (1: 1) are omitted in a number of important manuscripts, and this has led many to suppose that the Epistle was not intended for Ephesus alone, but for all the churches of the Lycus valley, of which the church at Ephesus was the chief.

It was God's purpose from before the foundation of the world to form a people for Himself. But mankind fell into sin and death, and only when Christ came was it revealed that God's purpose was to find accomplishment through the creation of a new humanity in Christ, made up of both Jew and Gentile, reconciled to God and to one another through the blood of the cross, and indwelt by the Holy Spirit. This 'new man' consists of the whole redeemed community of which Christ is the Head, and stands in contrast to the 'old man' whose head is Adam, and which is under the dominion of the world, the devil and the flesh, and is subject to divine condemnation.

This new humanity in Christ is the theme of the Epistle. The doctrine of individual salvation by faith, as expounded in Romans and Galatians, is here less prominent, and the apostle dwells rather upon the corporate aspects of salvation under the image of the church as the body of Christ, together with the vision of a final oneness of all things in Him.

Analysis

Theme: 'The New Humanity in Christ.'

1 – 3   God's purpose concerning His people.

☐ **STUDY 1   Ephesians 1: 1–14**

These verses deal with God's purpose to form a people for Himself and to sum up all things in Christ. Note the reiteration of 'in Christ' or 'in him'.

1   In verses 3–6 we are shown this people as conceived in the mind of God. What do we here learn concerning God's choice of us, His gifts to us, and His purpose for us? Do such thoughts immediately move us, as they moved Paul, to say 'Blessed be . . . God'? See Note 2 below.

2   In verses 7–14 we are shown this same people in process of redemption from sin. What parts are played in this work by (a) God the Father, (b) God the Son, and (c) God the Holy Spirit? Of what benefits are we here assured? What response is necessary on our part for their enjoyment?

Notes
1   Verse 3. 'In the heavenly places': a phrase emphasizing that the believer's blessings are spiritual, in contrast to the earthly and material blessings promised to Israel under the first covenant. *Cf.* Dt. 28: 8. The phrase occurs five times in this Epistle. See 1: 20; 2: 6; 3: 10; 6: 12. It refers to what today we might term 'the spirit realm', or 'the heavenly sphere'.
2   Verses 6, 12, 14. Note the recurring reference to 'the praise of his glory'. 'The design of redemption is to exhibit the grace of God in such a conspicuous manner as to fill all hearts with wonder and all lips with praise' (Charles Hodge).
3   Verse 13. 'Sealed': a mark of God's ownership.
4   Verse 14. 'Guarantee' or 'earnest' (AV, RV): a first instalment given as a pledge that all promised will be paid in full.

☐ **STUDY 2   Ephesians 1: 15–23**

1   What may we learn from this example concerning the way to pray for our fellow-Christians? When we do so, what ought to be our chief interest and concern? What are the three great spiritual truths which the apostle here prays that his readers may grasp?

2   Consider Christ's present position as set forth in verses 20–23 in relation to (a) God, (b) other powers and authorities, (c) the universe, and (d) the church. In the light of these verses has our conception of Christ been big enough?

Notes

1 Verse 18. 'His glorious inheritance in the saints': be careful to note that this is a reference not to our inheritance in Him but to His inheritance in us. *Cf.* Ex. 19: 5, 6; Tit. 2: 14.

2 Verses 22, 23. 'The church, . . . his body, the fulness of him': as God of old dwelt in the Temple and filled it with His glory, or as the fullness of the Godhead dwells in Jesus (Col. 1: 19; 2: 9, 10), so Christ now dwells in His church in His fullness. He fills it with His presence.

☐ **STUDY 3 Ephesians 2**

1 Verses 1–10. Work out the contrast between man's condition by nature and his position in Christ. What are we here said to be saved (a) from, and (b) for, or to enjoy? How has this amazing change been effected, and how does its enjoyment become ours?

2 Verses 11–22. Before Christ came, Jew and Gentile remained separate—kept apart in the Temple courts by a 'dividing wall' (verse 14). How did God deal with this situation through Christ's coming? What is now the position of believers, whether Jews or Gentiles, in relation to (a) God, and (b) one another? What three metaphors are used in verses 19–22 to show the complete equality of privilege which Gentile believers enjoy in Christ with those of Jewish birth?

Note. Verses 2, 3. 'Sons of disobedience', 'children of wrath': these phrases follow in their form Hebrew idioms. They describe those who are deliberately giving themselves to active rebellion against the will of God, and consequently are exposed to His active displeasure.

☐ **STUDY 4 Ephesians 3**

The apostle shows that the union of Jews and Gentiles in one body in Christ was in God's purpose from the beginning, though only now fully revealed to men.

1 Verses 1–13. What were Paul's personal calling and commission in relation to (a) the gospel, and (b) the Gentiles? Why was he chosen, and how was he qualified, for such service? Do you share his conviction that to suffer in such a cause is something to glory in rather than to be depressed about?

2 Verses 14–21. Trace the progressive stages in Paul's prayer for his readers. What blessings would its full answer bring into our lives? What guarantees that such an answer is more than possible? What ought we also to learn concerning the way to pray for our fellow-Christians?

3 What are the things included in the eternal purpose of God in Christ, in which Paul and all members of Christ's church are called to share? How may we more fully enter into our calling?

Notes

1 Verse 1. *Cf.* 6: 19, 20. Paul knew that his imprisonment was in the will of God, and in the interests of the truth and the spread of the gospel.

2 Verses 2 and 9. 'Stewardship', 'plan': Greek *oikonomia*. The word refers originally to household management. In verse 9 (*cf.* 1: 10), the reference is to God's administration, to His working out of His purpose in Christ. In verse 2, it is used of Paul's part in this—*i.e.*, of the special commission assigned to Paul. *Cf.* 1 Cor. 9: 16, 17.

3 Verses 3, 4, 9. 'The mystery': *i.e.*, divine truth hidden from natural discovery by men, but now specially revealed by the Spirit—particularly here the full content of God's plan for men's salvation.

☐ **STUDY 5 Ephesians 4: 1 – 5: 2**

1 Express in your own words the difference between the unity described in 4: 3–7, as already existing among Christians, and that mentioned in 4: 13–16, which Christians are to seek. How is the first to be preserved and how is the second to be attained?

2 From 4: 25 – 5: 2 list the things which must be put away, and those which ought to take their place. Notice also in each case the reason given by the apostle why we must live thus.

3 In what ways does Paul's fourfold description of the life of the Gentile world (4: 17–19) apply to the life of the non-Christian today? In contrast, what three principles are to govern the behaviour of Christians (4: 20–24)?

Notes

1 Verse 7. 'Grace': used here, as also in 3: 2, 8, of God's gifts to His people in Christ in appointing them to His special work. *Cf.* Mk. 13: 34; Mt. 25: 14, 15.

2 Verse 12 should be read with the first comma omitted, 'for the equipment of the saints for the work of ministry'.

3 Verses 22–24. The tenses in the Greek show that the 'putting off' of the old man and 'putting on' of the new are definite acts, whereas the 'being renewed' is a process. The living of this new Christian life is made possible for us through the continual renewing of the Spirit, enabling our minds to lay hold of the truth in Christ.

4 Verses 26, 27. While there may be anger which is not sin, anger is dangerous. It may lead to some action which gives the devil scope to strike a blow at the body of Christ.

☐ **STUDY 6 Ephesians 5: 3 – 6: 9**

1 5: 3–20. What are the positive motives and guiding principles of worthy Christian action, which the apostle here emphasizes? Add further items to your list (from Study 5) of actions, words and thoughts which ought (a) to be abandoned, and (b) to be expressed. Test your own life in this light. Why is constant watchfulness so necessary? What help does God give to make such living possible?

2   5: 21 – 6: 9. The opening verse states a governing principle. Consider how it is here applied to the common personal relations of everyday life—particularly those of wives, children and servants. What are the distinctive complementary responsibilities of husbands, parents and masters? Particularly notice in each case how the person concerned is in his (or her) action to relate himself (or herself) to Christ.

3   5: 23–32. Study in detail what we are here told concerning the relation between Christ and His church. What is the goal in view? How is it reached and realized?

Notes

1   5: 14. Paul is here possibly quoting from a Christian hymn, addressed to those who have not yet believed in Christ. *Cf.* Is. 60: 1.

2   5: 26. 'The washing of water with the word': here some simply compare Jn. 15: 2; 17: 17, but the majority recognize a reference to baptism. 'The word' may then refer to (a) the gospel preached, *cf.* Lk. 24: 27; (b) the formula used in Christian baptism, *cf.* Mt. 28: 19; or (c) the answering confession of the person being baptized, *cf.* 1 Pet. 3: 21, AV; Rom. 10: 9.

3   5: 32. 'A great mystery': the word 'great' here does not indicate that this truth is something 'very mysterious', but that this 'mystery' or 'divinely-revealed truth' is one 'of great importance'.

☐   **STUDY 7   Ephesians 6: 10–24**

The same apostle and Epistle that show us how heavenly, complete and free is redemption in Christ, now indicate how certain, fierce and protracted is the conflict to be faced by those who belong to Christ.

1   Why is conflict inevitable for all who belong to Christ? What is its character? What dangers which beset us are here particularly in mind? *Cf.* 2 Cor. 10: 3–5; 11: 3. By what achievement is victory here repeatedly described? How alone may it be achieved?

2   Some interpreters take 'truth' to mean inward sincerity and 'righteousness' to mean integrity and fidelity. Others think 'truth' here means the truth of the gospel, as in 4: 21, and take 'righteousness' to mean 'the righteousness of God' given to us in Christ (see Rom. 3: 22). Can you find a decisive answer? How alone can we make our standing sure before God, men and the devil? *Cf.* Rom. 5: 1, 2; 8: 33, 34; Pss. 15; 24: 3–6; 51: 6.

3   Verses 18–20. Consider what is here implied about Christian praying—concerning its place, its character, its demands, its scope, and its particular interests and requests. Measure your praying by these standards.

Notes

1   Verse 10. 'Be strong': literally 'be strengthened'. 'A person cannot strengthen himself; he must be empowered' (*Ephesians* (*TNTC*), p. 170). Our strength is to be continually maintained (present tense) by the outworked vigour of God's inherent power.

2   Verses 11, 13. 'The whole armour of God': the complete outfit is thought of as one whole. What is most emphasized is its divine source.

3   Verse 12. The word for 'contending', literally 'to wrestle' (see AV, RV), implies personal hand-to-hand conflict.

4   Verse 15. For such fighting one needs to have a sure foothold.

5   Verse 16. 'Flaming darts': devil-inspired thoughts or desires, evil in their nature, and tending to inflame the passions.

JOB

Introduction

Outside the book itself, Job, the chief character, is mentioned only in Ezk. 14: 14, 20 and Jas. 5: 11. We know very little about him therefore, and the date and the placing of the story are matters of surmise. All absence of clear links with the patriarchal or post-conquest Israel point to an early date, and it is reasonable to take the descriptions of scenery and climate as referring to a country on the western edge of the desert. The book is written in Hebrew by a Hebrew.

We are given a portrait of a good man suddenly overtaken by extraordinary disasters. The main action of the book lies in a series of speeches between Job, his three friends, the young man Elihu, and, in the end, God Himself. In these speeches interest is sustained throughout by the presentation of opposing ideas about Job's misfortunes. Sharp divergences of temperament and belief reveal themselves. The friends insist that suffering comes only when a man has sinned. So let Job repent and his restoration will follow immediately. But Job knows that he has not sinned, at least not so greatly as to deserve so devastating a punishment. The principal agony lies, not in his diseased body, but in his bewildered mind. His cry to God to explain Himself is maintained with growing impatience. Job's real trial is theological. For he, like his friends, had once believed that men suffer here for their sins.

At last his desire is granted. God speaks to him, but very differently from his expectation. The sole divine answer consists of a vision of God's great power. Job, seeing his small concerns against this vast back-cloth, is humbled and silenced. Then God commends him, and he is restored.

The book is usually considered to be an enquiry into the reasons for innocent suffering, with Elihu seeing furthest into its meaning and purpose. Suffering is a merciful deterrent, aimed at reforming. Yet, from the standpoint of the Prologue, it is disinterested goodness which is under discussion. Satan asks, 'Does Job fear God for nought?' implying that he fears God because he has been weighed down with wealth and possessions. Job then, by divine permission, becomes a test case, to see whether he does fear God for the inducements to do so which he gets from it. Stripped of family, wealth, health, reputation and friends, he emerges at last from the experiment unscathed and believing God when all comforting proofs of His presence had been withdrawn.

Perhaps this book also teaches in a limited way how God justifies a man who has faith. He does it, not by explaining to him why life is as it is, still less by vindicating his alleged sinlessness. He does it by a personal showing of Himself to the man who cries for Him to hear, and clings to the hope of a revelation. And in that marvellous vision of power with which the book ends, totally unexpected, yet coherent and convincing as it is, Job, like Thomas before the risen Christ, is delivered from his doubt, and bows in worship. God, in showing Himself to a faithful man, in the very act justifies him. Revelation in response to faith is justification. Job was 'right', but not for the reasons he supposed.

The study of the subordinate themes in the book is well worth the time. Job's preoccupation with death, for example, and his hopes of an after-life; his certainty that somewhere a mediator will be found; his irony, his reactions to his suffering, and his character; the characters, too, of his friends, so full of truths, so far from the truth. To these, and other matters, attention is drawn in the Notes and the Questions.

Analysis

1, 2	Of the happy and exemplary life of Job. Why and how he suffered.
3	Job complains, and wishes that he had never been born.
4 – 14	The first cycle of speeches.
15 – 21	The second cycle of speeches.
22 – 31	The third cycle of speeches.

32 – 37	The speeches of Elihu.
38: 1 – 42: 6	The speeches of the Lord and Job's replies. Job regrets having questioned God's goodness.
42: 7 – 17	After Job has prayed for his friends, he is commended by God and given twice as much as before.

☐ STUDY 1 Job 1 – 3

1   1: 1 – 2: 6. What is said here about Job's (a) character, (b) position in life, and (c) sufferings?

2   2: 7 – 3: 26. In 2: 10 Job expresses his faith in God. In 3: 11 he wants to die; and in 3: 23 blames God for his troubles. How are we to account for this change?

Notes
1   2: 13. The seven-day silence of Job's friends is a rite of mourning for a man they consider as good as dead, struck down because of his sins.
2   Compare 3: 1-26 with Je. 20: 14-18.

The First Cycle of Speeches (4 – 14)

The three friends, seeing Job's suffering, assume his guilt, and with mounting zeal urge him to repent. At first Job is only grieved and hurt by this lack of understanding, but soon becomes irritated and angry. He wants God to explain Himself, and is acutely miserable.

☐ STUDY 2 Job 4 and 5. Eliphaz' first speech

1   4: 1-11. According to Eliphaz, what was Job forgetting?

2   4: 12 – 5: 7. What did Eliphaz learn from his vision?

3   5: 8-27. What is his view of Job, of God, and of divine chastening?

Notes
1   5: 2. 'Vexation': an impatient, querulous or presumptuous attitude.
2   5: 6, 7. Troubles in life come as sparks come, from somebody's actions. There must be a human cause. *Cf.* 4: 8.
3   5: 27. An appeal to scholarly research to buttress his orthodoxy.

☐ STUDY 3 Job 6 and 7. Job's reply to Eliphaz

Job is hurt by Eliphaz' attitude. He had hoped for help, not criticism (6: 14). He flings questions at God.

1   6: 1-30. What does Job's condition make him long for (a) from God, and (b) from men? What may we learn from his double disappointment?

2   7: 1-10. By what metaphors does Job describe his present life?
7: 11-21. What is the substance of his complaints against God?

Notes
1 6: 5, 6. Even animals cry out in misery: and human beings exclaim at distasteful food. Why shouldn't Job complain?
2 6: 20. Thirsty caravans perish in the desert pursuing a mirage. Job is similarly cheated by his friends.
3 6: 30. 'Cannot my taste . . .' means 'Am I quite without good reason for my complaints?'

☐ **STUDY 4   Job 8: 1 – 9: 24. Bildad's first speech and Job's reply**

1   To what authority does Bildad appeal for what he says? How trustworthy do you think that authority is? What are Bildad's views (a) about God, and (b) about wicked men?

2   What difficulties does Job find in his way as he tries to make God explain Himself?

Notes
1 8: 4. A cruel remark. Job's children died because they sinned, according to Bildad.
2 8: 11. Reeds wither without water. So wicked men fade away.
3 9: 2. The meaning is, 'How can a man establish his righteousness before God?'
4 9: 13b. Rahab is probably another name for the dragon. See RSV mg. note to 9: 8b.

☐ **STUDY 5   Job 9: 25 – 10: 22. Job's reply to Bildad (continued)**

1   9: 33. The 'umpire' is mentioned for the first time in the book. Keep a list of the occurrences, noticing what new features each fresh mention brings. Suggest ways in which Jesus Christ has made Job's great wish a reality for us.

2   What is Job's main desire in chapter 10? Do you think God is angered by such plain speaking? *Cf.* Pss. 55: 1–8, 22; 62: 8.

Notes
1 9: 35. 'Deep in my heart I have no guilty fears.'
2 10: 12. An extraordinary verse to find in a long complaint. Either it means 'Even in deep misery I am aware of an overriding loving purpose'; or 'Even my past happiness was designed as a prelude to my present misery.'

☐ **STUDY 6   Job 11 and 12. Zophar's first speech and Job's reply**

1   Observe (a) the sharp rebuke in 11: 6; (b) the steps to repentance in 11: 13, 14; (c) the picture of blessing in 11: 15–19. Why do you think Zophar failed to help Job?

2   Eliphaz spoke of visions, and research, Bildad of the wisdom of the ancients. To what authority does Zophar appeal to support his conviction that sin and suffering are inevitably linked?

3   Zophar and Job each speak of divine wisdom. Compare the various examples of it which they cite.

Note. 12: 5–12. Perhaps Job is ironically quoting Zophar's views back at him. Job's point is that these platitudes are irrelevant to his situation. He does not deny them.

☐   **STUDY 7   Job 13 and 14. Job speaks again**

For convenience the first cycle has been considered as ending at 14. It could equally finish at 12, with 13 and 14 beginning the fresh round of opposing speeches.

1   What is Job's chief accusation against his friends? What two demands does he now make to God?

2   In the long dirge on man's uncertainties in chapter 14 there is one small but significant gleam of hope. What is it? Compare and contrast the Christian's view of this hope with Job's. (Note, however, that in chapter 18 Job relapses into a deeper pessimism still.)

The Second Cycle of Speeches (15 – 21)

Unable to persuade Job that he is wrong, his friends now use blunter accusation and scarcely-veiled threats. They dwell on the fate of the wicked. Job, by this time very upset, sinks into repeated moanings about his troubles. Then, quite suddenly, at the deepest point of misery he revives a little (16: 19; 19: 25), and in 21 attacks this antique idea of his friends that 'It's always the bad who get the pain', and accuses them of preaching a dogma denied by life. Their observations are inaccurate.

☐   **STUDY 8   Job 15 – 17. Eliphaz' second speech and Job's reply**

1   Read chapter 15 and compare its tone and approach with Eliphaz' first speech in chapters 4 and 5. Note the emphasis on human depravity. How should Eliphaz have dealt with a younger man who would not agree with him? Why was he so sure he was right? To whose shortcomings was he blind?

2   16 and 17. Even in the depths, Job finds some particles of hope. What form do these take?

Notes
1   15: 4. Eliphaz accuses Job of being an enemy of true religion and godliness because he denies the traditional orthodoxy.
2   15: 11b. A reference to the earlier speeches of Job's friends.
3   15: 18, 19. Eliphaz claims that his doctrine is ancient and pure, untainted by foreign heresies.
4   16: 2. Ronald Knox renders this: 'Old tales and cold comfort; you are all alike.'

5 16: 19, 21. A further reference to the mediator.

6 17: 16b. Taken as a statement, not a question, this indicates a sudden further advance in Job's hopes.

☐ STUDY 9 Job 18 and 19. Bildad's second speech and Job's reply

1 In 18 trace the sequence of events which happen to the wicked and the ungodly.

2 In 19 Job says he feels imprisoned and alone. List the metaphors under which he pictures his solitary confinement. How does he picture his release? To what grand assurance does his faith triumphantly rise?

Notes

1 18: 2. 'How long before you make a capture of mere words?' *i.e.*, before you stop mouthing empty ideas. 'Consider': *i.e.*, say something worth saying, and our answer will be weighty.

2 18: 4. The world's natural laws will not be altered to suit Job.

3 19: 25–27. Even if Job had no hope of vindication in this life he believed that God must vindicate him and that, after death, he would see God and find God on his side. *Cf.* Rom. 8: 33–39.

4 19: 28b. 'The real cause of the trouble is himself' possibly expresses the sense intended.

5 19: 29. 'Trouble will come to them if they go on rejecting his cries for pity' is what Job here means.

☐ STUDY 10 Job 20 and 21. Zophar's second speech and Job's reply

1 Place Zophar's views of the state of the wicked in this world alongside Job's. *Cf.* 20: 6–28 with 21: 6–26. At what points do they (a) agree, and (b) disagree?

2 In this second cycle Job's friends, gaining no victory, utter threats. Is defeated conservatism bound to take refuge in acid predictions of gloom? Had Job something to teach them if only they were willing to learn?

Notes

1 20: 5. *Cf.* Pss. 37 and 73 on the sudden end of bad men.

2 20: 7. 'Dead men are dead.' Job's hopes about another life receive short measure from Zophar.

3 20: 17. 'The rivers': *i.e.*, of paradise.

4 21: 34. Job means that they have not troubled to check their thesis against life itself. So they are dealing in lies.

Concluding note to the section chapters 15–21. Job's friends have nothing new to say: but Job has. He is stumbling towards the truth that death itself will provide a way out of his impasse, when a shadowy but friendly Redeemer will acquit him.

The Third Cycle of Speeches (22 – 31)

Only Eliphaz speaks at length to Job in this third cycle. Zophar says nothing (see, however, the Note on 27: 7–22). The friends' case against Job is already leaking badly. Eliphaz sinks it by shouting false charges at Job, which Job later (31) refutes. Job ends by repeating his innocence, and his perplexity.

☐ **STUDY 11 Job 22 – 24. Eliphaz' third speech and Job's reply**

1 Chapter 22. Of what does Eliphaz accuse Job (verses 6–9)? List God's blessings on the humble (verses 21–30). Why does Eliphaz' list of blessings (verse 3) make so little impression on Job?

2 Chapter 23. Job earnestly desires to find God (verse 3). How is he now thinking of God? See verses 5, 6, 10, 13, 16. Is it as a Friend or a Foe?

3 Chapter 24. What anomalies does Job see in society around him? Compare what 'you' say (verses 18–20) with what Job says. Does this chapter teach us anything about how to make observations on life?

Note. 22: 2–4. Eliphaz' argument is that God's treatment of man is not with a view to any gain or advantage to Himself but for man's sake. Since we cannot suppose that He punishes them for their piety (verse 4), it must be because of their sin.

☐ **STUDY 12 Job 25 – 27. Bildad's third speech and Job's reply**

1 How do Bildad and Job speak of (a) God's holiness, and (b) His omnipotence?

2 The knowledge of God's power does not help Job now. To what does he cling (27: 1–6)? Was he right in this?

3 Does 27: 7–22 add any fresh ideas about the wicked?

Note. 27: 7–22. Some part of the otherwise lost third speech of Zophar is possibly here. The thought echoes 20: 12ff.

☐ **STUDY 13 Job 28 and 29. The search for wisdom: Job's final speech**

1 Chapter 28. What is here expressed concerning (a) human skill, and (b) human inability? What are (a) the source, and (b) the essence of true wisdom? *Cf.* 1: 1; 2: 3; Ps. 34: 11–14.

2 Chapter 29. What may we learn from Job's description of his manner of life before tragedy overwhelmed him? What most stands

out in his memory? What then gave enrichment and direction to his daily living?

Notes

1 Chapter 28 reads like an independent insertion—a poem in praise of wisdom. The 'wisdom' meant is not simply mental ability, but understanding of the right way to act in the face of life's mystery. Supremely, as known only to God, it means the master plan behind the created order. The New Testament declares that this wisdom is found and expressed in Christ. *Cf.* 1 Cor. 1: 30; Col. 2: 23.

2 Job's speech in chapters 29–31 is best understood as a concluding monologue, summing up the whole situation.

STUDY 14   Job 30 and 31. Job's final speech (continued)

1   Chapter 30. Contrast Job's present condition with his previous prosperity surveyed in chapter 29. In what different ways is Job now beset by misery and distress? What is his chief reason for perplexity and complaint?

2   Chapter 31. Of what sins, secret and public, does Job here declare himself innocent? Make a list and use it for self-examination. In contrast to the judgment of his friends, what is Job here seeking to prove about his present condition?

The Speeches of Elihu (32 – 37)

STUDY 15   Job 32 and 33. The introduction and first speech of Elihu

Elihu is a young man who has overheard the friends and Job speaking. Both sides anger him, and he wants to put things right. His main beliefs are these: God is incapable of making a mistake; pain is a divine deterrent aimed at keeping men from sin.

1   What made Elihu angry? On what grounds does he claim a right to speak? What do you think of the way he begins his speech?

2   Job had said that God treated him unjustly (33: 8–11), and that He made matters worse by refusing to talk to him (33: 13). What replies does Elihu give to Job about this? See verses 12, 14–33. In what ways does he say God speaks? And for what purpose?

STUDY 16   Job 34 and 35. Elihu's second speech

1   According to Elihu Job says (a) that God is wronging him (34: 5, 6), and (b) that there is no profit to be gained from delighting in God and doing His will (34: 9; 35: 3). How does Elihu answer these contentions? What precious truths about God does he declare?

2 'In the setting of the book of Job it is not a question whether Elihu is right or not—obviously he is right, at least in large measure —but whether he contributes anything to the solution of Job's "Why?" Obviously he does not' (H. L. Ellison). Do you agree with this judgment? Why did a man who knew so much fail to be helpful? Of what danger should this make us aware?

Notes

1 34: 13–15. The thought here seems to be that God as Creator has no motive for injustice; and that the existence and preservation of the universe is an evidence of God's interest in His creatures.

2 34: 23–30. There is no need for God to act as men do by process of trial and judgment. God knows all and acts at once.

3 35: 10. God is the only source of all true comfort. *Cf.* Ps. 42: 8; 2 Cor. 1: 3, 4.

☐ **STUDY 17   Job 36 and 37. Elihu's last speech**

1 What does Elihu here assert concerning (a) the character of God's rule, and (b) the evidences of His greatness? To what conclusion about his troubles does he seek to lead Job?

2 Of what is Elihu profoundly aware concerning (a) the character and the ways of God, and (b) his own attempts to describe them? *Cf.* Rom. 11: 33–36.

Note. 37: 20. Elihu expresses dread at the thought of contending with God.

The Speeches of the Lord and Job's Replies (38: 1 – 42: 6)

☐ **STUDY 18   Job 38: 1 – 40: 5. The first speech of the Lord and Job's reply**

1 Consider the examples of God's handiwork here depicted. What relation had this to Job's condition and perplexity? What response ought this to produce in us? *Cf.* Pss. 97: 1–6, 12; 104: 1, 24.

2 Job had pleaded for an interview with God in which his innocence could be established. See 13: 3; 23: 3, 4; 31: 37. God proves his littleness. Why do you think Job is answered like this? What does Job confess in his reply?

Notes

1 38: 2. This means: 'You are obscuring the truth by speaking without thinking.'

2 38: 4ff. The reader should take good note of the bold, magnificent images employed here. The world is like a building erected by one man (verse 4). The sea's birth was like a child's issuing from the womb (verse 8). Dawn shakes the earth like an open-air sleeper rising and shaking out of his blanket the

creatures which came in for warmth (verses 12, 13). 'God is now speaking to deeper need, to the hidden fear, hardly realized by Job and certainly uncon-fessed, that there might be somewhere where the writ of God did not run, where God was not all-sovereign' (H. L. Ellison).

3 30: 2. This means: 'Can you prove yourself right only by proving me wrong?'

☐ **STUDY 19 Job 40: 6 – 42: 6. The Lord's second speech and Job's reply**

1 God brings before Job two powerful wild creatures—the hippo-potamus (40: 15–24) and the crocodile (41: 1–34). What does God intend that Job should learn from these animals? What questions does He ask Job?

2 Job has been given no explanation of his sufferings. What brought him to the deep humbling and self-abasement described in 42: 1–6?

Note. 'The point in these descriptions is the prodigality of Created Might' (H. R. Minn).

☐ **STUDY 20 Job 42: 7–17. The Epilogue**

1 Job's friends would certainly have agreed with all that God said to Job. Yet God is angry with them. 'You have not', He says, 'spoken of me what is right' (verse 7). Why was this so? Was it their haste in condemning Job, their doctrinal prejudice, their lack of sympathy, or what was it?

2 Job had quarrelled with God, doubted His justice, insisted on his own innocence, wanted to end his life. Yet God said he had spoken 'what is right'. Why?

☐ **STUDY 21 Revision: Job 1–42**

Re-read your notes on the main teaching of the book of Job. What have you learnt about (a) the origin and purpose of suffering, or so-called 'evil' (42: 11); (b) the way to bear it; and (c) the way to help others to bear it?

PSALMS 42 - 51

☐ **STUDY 36   Psalms 42 and 43**

These two psalms were probably originally one. Notice the thrice-repeated refrain (42: 5, 11; 43: 5).

1   What phrase does the psalmist repeat four times in these two psalms to describe his spiritual condition? What were the chief causes of his sorrow, and what his chief desire?

2   What can we learn from the psalmist's example as to how to deal with depression in our lives?

☐ **STUDY 37   Psalm 44**

A national appeal to God in a time of great suffering.

1   What does the psalmist say about (a) God's dealings in the past on behalf of His people, and (b) His relationship with them? See verses 1–8. In spite of past happenings, what seems to be the situation at the present time? See verses 9–22.

2   What can we learn from this psalm as to what we should do when it seems as if God has deserted us? *Cf.* Is. 50: 10; Lk. 18: 1.

☐ **STUDY 38   Psalm 45**

A marriage song of a king. If the king be a type of Christ (see Heb. 1: 8, 9), the bride may symbolize the church.

1   What features in Christ's character are here portrayed?

2   How can we apply to ourselves the counsel given to the bride concerning the winning of the king's favour?

☐ **STUDY 39   Psalms 46 – 48**

These psalms are a trilogy of praise in memory of a great deliverance, most probably that of Jerusalem from the king of Assyria. They should be read in the light of 2 Ki. 18 and 19.

1   Gather out what is said about God in these psalms: His power, His character, His relation to the world, and His relation to His own people.

2   What is the leading thought of each of the three psalms? What should be the response of God's people to such a manifestation of His power and love?

Notes
1   46: 5. 'Right early': better, 'When the morning dawns', *i.e.*, the morning of deliverance. See RV mg. and *cf.* Mk. 6: 48, 51.
2   47: 2 and 48: 2. 'The great King': *i.e.*, the true great king in contrast to the Assyrian monarch, who bore this title. *Cf.* Is. 36: 4.
3   47: 10. 'Shields': meaning 'rulers'. *Cf.* Ps. 89: 18. The verse is prophetic of Christ's final victory. *Cf.* 1 Cor. 15: 24, 25; Rev. 15: 3, 4.

☐   **STUDY 40   Psalm 49**

An inspired meditation, addressed to all men, on the vanity of riches. It anticipates our Lord's teaching in Lk. 12: 13-21.

1   How do men in general regard wealth? See verses 6, 13, 18. But what are the facts? What can wealth *not* do (verses 7-9)? And what is the end of the rich man (verses 10-14, 17-20)?

2   Why is it better to trust in God than in riches? See verses 14, 15. And what is the psalmist's counsel to himself and to us? See verses 5 and 16.

Note. Verses 7 and 9 should be read together, verse 8 being parenthetical. With verse 7 *cf.* Ex. 21: 30. There were cases where, in human relationships, life could be redeemed with money; but it is not so when God summons the soul.

☐   **STUDY 41   Psalm 50**

A picture of God's judgment of His people. There are four sections: (a) Introduction (verses 1-6); (b) God speaks to His people (verses 7-15); (c) God speaks to the wicked (verses 16-21); (d) Epilogue (verses 22, 23).

1   What can you discover of God's character in His capacity as Judge in verses 1-6? What further truth about Him is emphasized in verses 7-13?

2   What does God require of His people if they are to please Him, and what benefits does He promise to them? See verses 14, 15, 23. In what ways do the wicked displease God, and what is their end compared to those who fulfil His requirements?

☐   **STUDY 42   Psalm 51**

Note the occasion of the psalm, as given in the title.

1   What may we learn about confession and the grounds of for-

giveness from verses 1–5? Note (a) the terms which David uses to describe himself and his wrongdoing, and (b) where his hope lies.

2   David realizes that his whole nature is sinful, and that God requires sincerity and integrity in the innermost part of his being (verse 6; cf. 1 Sa. 16: 7). What, therefore, (in verses 7–12) does he ask for in addition to forgiveness? Also what does he promise shall be the outcome of God's answer to his prayer? See verses 13–17.

Note. Verse 4. This does not mean that David had not also done wrong against man (note in verse 14 his confession of 'bloodguiltiness'), but that he now saw his wrongdoing in this one outstanding aspect of it, as being sin against God. Cf. Gn. 39: 9; 2 Sa. 12: 13.

For Studies 43–56 on the Psalms see p. 239.

---

2 SAMUEL

For Introduction, see p. 208.

Analysis

1 – 8   David consolidates his position and takes Jerusalem.
9 – 12   David the king, to the time of his great sin.
13 – 20   The punishment of sin: Absalom's rebellion.
21 – 24   An appendix containing other historical incidents and summaries, and David's last words.

☐ **STUDY 1   2 Samuel 1**

1   The Amalekite thought he was bringing David good news (cf. 2 Sa. 4: 10), but he had mistaken his man. Why did David have him killed?

2 What light does this episode, and the lament for Saul and Jonathan (verses 19–27), throw on David's character? Bearing in mind the faults of the king to whom David was so loyal, are there any lessons here for me?

☐ **STUDY 2   2 Samuel 2 and 3**

1 Compare David's actions as a public figure (2: 4–7; 3: 20, 21, 28–39) with the trouble he was building up in his family life (3: 2–5, 13, 14). Am I in any respect guilty of double standards in my own life?

2 Make a character study of the figures of Abner and Joab from these chapters. Note the relationship of Joab and his brothers to David (Zeruiah was the daughter of David's mother by her first marriage), and David's words in 3: 39.

☐ **STUDY 3   2 Samuel 4: 1 – 5: 16**

1 In what respects was the crime of Rechab and Baanah worse than that of the Amalekite?

2 David waited for seven years for the decision at the beginning of chapter 5. Why did the Israelites now choose him as king? *Cf.* Dt. 17: 15.

3 How did David succeed in taking the stronghold of Zion, and why?

☐ **STUDY 4   2 Samuel 5: 17 – 6: 23**

1 Why was it David won these two battles with the Philistines?

2 Why did Uzzah die? *Cf.* 1 Sa. 6: 19; Nu. 4: 15; 1 Ch. 15: 15. What was God teaching through this incident?

3 What was the real reason for Michal's contempt for David, and what her pretended reason? Why was it David behaved as he did on this occasion? Can I learn anything from his exuberance 'before the Lord'?

☐ **STUDY 5   2 Samuel 7**

1 David is eager to build a house for God—God's reply is to make a 'house' for David. List what He has already done, and what He promises for the future.

2 It has been said that what a man is on his knees before God, that he really is. What does David's prayer reveal (a) about himself, (b) about his relation to God?

☐ **STUDY 6   2 Samuel 8 and 9**

1   Use a map to follow the path of David's victories. What reasons does the writer emphasize for David's success?

2   How does David's treatment of the spoils of war differ from the way in which he dealt with the gods of the Philistines captured in battle (1 Ch. 14: 8–12)? Is there a reason for this? *Cf.* Dt. 7: 5.

3   Do you see any parallel between David's treatment of Mephibosheth and God's acceptance of us?

☐ **STUDY 7   2 Samuel 10 and 11**

1   Why is Hanun's treatment of David's envoys inexcusable?

2   Joab shows up in a better light here. What does this add to what we already know of his character?

3   At what stage in his career did David fall? Where should he have been at the time? How did the temptation grow? Was he able to keep his sin secret? Do your answers to these questions, and your reading of the passage, suggest any general lessons about sin?

☐ **STUDY 8   2 Samuel 12: 1 – 13: 37**

1   How did God open David's eyes to his sin through Nathan's words? Are you prepared for Him similarly to open your eyes?

2   What may we learn from chapter 12 about (a) repentance, (b) forgiveness, and (c) discipline? *Cf.* Ps. 33: 3–5; Heb. 12: 6, 11.

3   13: 1–37. What lessons emerge from a comparison of Amnon's sin with David's? What was wrong with the way in which Amnon was treated by (a) David, and (b) Absalom?

☐ **STUDY 9   2 Samuel 13: 38 – 14: 33**

1   What is laudable in the actions here recorded of (a) Joab and (b) David, and what gives rise to misgivings?

2   How does David's predicament illustrate the situation confronting God with the human race? How is the gospel 'solution' at once more far-reaching and more satisfactory than the expedient adopted by David?

3   Study Absalom's character, and list his faults.

Note. 14: 7. Those who demanded the murderer's death had justification according to the law (see Dt. 19: 11–13). The woman based her plea on her own great need.

☐ **STUDY 10   2 Samuel 15: 1 – 16: 14**

1   How was it that Absalom 'stole the hearts of the men of Israel'? What do you make of David's reactions here?

2   Contrast the behaviour of Absalom with that of Ittai and Hushai.

3   Consider how the rebellion shows certain men in their true colours (16: 1–14). Again note David's reactions.

☐ **STUDY 11   2 Samuel 16: 15 – 17: 29**

1   What are the reasons for Ahitophel's first piece of advice to Absalom? What do you think would have been David's first thought (*cf.* 12: 11, 12)? Is this the key to David's rather defeatist attitude?

2   17: 1–14. Was Ahitophel's counsel good? If so, why was it that Hushai's advice won the day?

3   How was David rewarded for his previous generosity? Notice who Shobi was (see 2 Sa. 10: 12).

☐ **STUDY 12   2 Samuel 18: 1 – 19: 8**

1   What is good and what is bad about David's concern for Absalom?

2   Consider Joab's conduct throughout this passage, separating the good and bad points.

☐ **STUDY 13   2 Samuel 19: 9–39**

1   Why did David not make an immediate re-entry into the capital? How does his attitude contrast with that of Saul and other leaders in the same mould? See 1 Sa. 8: 10–18.

2   What qualities in David stand out in his treatment of (a) Shimei, (b) Mephibosheth, and (c) Barzillai? What can be learnt from the attitude of each of these men to David?

Note. Verse 11. The fact that Absalom's rebellion centred in Hebron (15: 7–12) shows how deeply the tribe of Judah was implicated in it.

☐ **STUDY 14   2 Samuel 19: 40 – 20: 26**

1   Analyse the quarrel between Israel and Judah: (a) its cause; (b) the arguments used; (c) the spirit in which it was conducted; (d) its tragic outcome.

2   How was the threatened disaster averted? What part was played respectively by David, by Joab, and by the wise woman in the town of Abel?

3   What considerations aggravate Joab's sin in murdering Amasa? *Cf.* 2 Sa. 17: 25; 19: 13.

☐ **STUDY 15   2 Samuel 21**

1   Why was Saul's attempt to exterminate the Gibeonites wrong? How was David careful not to make the same mistake? Do we stand by our word? *Cf.* Ps. 15: 4c.

2   There was a law that those who were hanged were to be buried the same day. What was the reason for this law? *Cf.* Dt. 21: 23. How does it explain the exception that is made here?

3   What significance is there in the fact that giants troubled David right to the end of his life?

Note. Verse 19. *Cf.* 1 Ch. 20: 5 which seems to have preserved more accurately the original text.

☐ **STUDY 16   2 Samuel 22**

See Psalm 18 for questions already set on this psalm.

1   Are there any passages in this psalm which we could not echo as Christians?

2   Does the psalm bring to mind any particular incidents recorded in 2 Samuel?

☐ **STUDY 17   2 Samuel 23**

1   Compare verses 3 and 4 with verse 5. What apparent conflict is there between the two reasons given by David for his happiness and prosperity? Is this conflict real? *Cf.* Phil. 2: 12, 13.

2   What light is cast on verses 6 and 7 by David's advice to Solomon in 1 Ki. 2: 5, 6? *Cf.* 1 Ki. 2: 31–33.

3   Consider what David's followers were willing to do for their king; and at what stage in his career (verse 13). What lessons are there here for a Christian?

☐ **STUDY 18   2 Samuel 24**

1   (a) Compare the length of time taken by Joab to count, and by the angel to slay the Israelites. (b) Compare the atonement required by God for David's adultery (2 Sa. 12: 15, 18) with that exacted

here. What sin on David's part is being dealt with? What two lessons are taught about it? *Cf.* Pr. 16: 5.

2 Where was Araunah's threshing-floor? See Note on verse 16. What outstanding event had happened there previously? See Gn. 22: 2. What was the site eventually used for?

3 Is there a lesson for us in David's declaration of verse 24?

Note. Verse 16. We learn from 2 Ch. 3: 1 that Araunah's threshing-floor was on Mount Moriah, which became the site of the Temple.

PSALMS 52 - 72

☐ **STUDY 43** **Psalms 52-54**

Of these three psalms the second (Ps. 53) is a duplicate (with slight variations) of Ps. 14. For the occasion of Pss. 52 and 54 see their titles and *cf.* 1 Sa. 22: 9; 23: 19.

1 52: 1-7; 53: 1-5. How is the godless man described? In what does he put his trust, and what is his end? In what does the godly man put his trust, and what is the result for him? See 52: 8, 9; 53: 6.

2 What may we learn from Ps. 54 of (a) the severity of faith's trial; (b) the ground of faith's confidence; (c) faith's assurance of triumph?

☐ **STUDY 44** **Psalm 55**

1 Of the two ways of meeting trouble mentioned in verses 6, 7 and 22 respectively, which is the better? What other verses show that the psalmist is turning to God for help, rather than seeking to escape from the scene of his distress?

2 What was the bitterest element in the psalmist's grief? See verses 12-14, 21 and *cf.* 2 Sa. 15: 31; Jn. 13: 21. Observe, however, the difference between David's cry in verse 15, and our Lord's word concerning Judas (Mk. 14: 21).

Notes
1 Verses 9–11. Violence, strife, iniquity, mischief, wickedness, oppression, fraud, seem to be personified as walking on the walls and in the streets of the city.
2 Verse 22. 'Your burden': the Hebrew word translated 'burden' means literally 'what he has given you'. See RSV mg. The thought seems to be, 'Take back to God, and cast upon Him the burden He has laid upon you, and He will sustain you under it. For He has given it to you to bring you to Himself.' *Cf.* Ps. 107: 23–30.

☐ **STUDY 45 Psalms 56 and 57**

These two psalms are closely connected and, according to their titles, should be read against the background of 1 Sa. 21: 10 – 22: 1.

1 In these two psalms how does David (a) describe the trials by which he is surrounded, and (b) express his confidence in God?

2 What does David confess that God has done, and can do, for him, and in what ways does he say that he will show his gratitude? How far can you make some of the words of these psalms your own?

Note. Ps. 56: 8. *Cf.* Mt. 10: 30.

☐ **STUDY 46 Psalms 58 and 59**

1 Ps. 58. When earthly rulers pervert justice and 'deal out violence', what can the righteous do? What will prove to them that 'there is a God who judges on earth'? Notice the vivid imagery in verses 6–9.

2 Ps. 59. Make a list of the different ways in which David here addresses God. How are the truths of the previous psalm here applied more personally to the psalmist's own circumstances? Can you make some similar personal application?

☐ **STUDY 47 Psalm 60**

For the occasion of this psalm see the title and 2 Sa. 8: 13, 14. The circumstances are not wholly clear. It would seem that while David was engaged in a campaign against Syria (Aram), the Edomites invaded Judah from the south, creating a situation of grave danger. The psalm was written when David first heard the news.

1 Note the content of David's prayer. What does he do first (verses 1–5), second (verses 6–8), third (verses 9–12)?

2 What may we learn from David's example concerning the way (a) to meet bad tidings, and (b) to find help in God?

Notes
1 Verse 6. Shechem west of the Jordan, Succoth east of it, thus representing the whole land.
2 Verse 8. 'Upon Edom': better, 'to Edom', as in RV mg. Moab and Edom were to have a menial place in God's household, as compared with Israel.

☐ **STUDY 48 Psalms 61 and 62**

Pss. 61–63 form another trilogy, like 46–48. They were all most probably written shortly after David's flight from Absalom (see 63 title) and should be read against the background of the story of 2 Sa. 15–17.

1 Ps. 61. Consider David's circumstances—a fugitive, his throne occupied by another, his life sought. What were his heart's chief desires, as expressed in his prayers (verses 1–4)? Observe also his confident hope, and his whole-hearted devotion (verses 5–8). Is he not in this a 'type' of our Lord?

2 Ps. 62. How did David's situation appear in the eyes of his enemies (verse 3), and how to the eye of faith (verses 6, 7)? Out of the fullness of his own joyous confidence in God, what message was David able to give his followers (verses 8–12)? Have you also found that faith leads to testimony?

Note. 62: 11, 12. 'Once . . . twice': a Hebrew idiom for 'repeatedly', here signifying that the truth David sets forth in these verses had sunk deep into his heart.

☐ **STUDY 49 Psalm 63**

The title of the psalm assigns it to the time when David was crossing the wilderness of Judah, *i.e.*, from Jerusalem to Jordan, in his flight from Absalom, as described in 2 Sa. 16. The psalm begins in a mournful way, but suddenly, at verse 2, the note changes, and the psalm becomes one of joyous praise. The most satisfactory explanation of the change, and of David's words '*So I have looked upon thee in the sanctuary*', is that there, in the wilderness, David was given a vision of Jehovah as vivid and glorious as ever he had seen Him in the sanctuary, and it transformed for him the whole outlook.

1 Consider how full of sorrow David's heart must have been at leaving Jerusalem, and especially the sanctuary of God. See verse 1, and *cf.* 2 Sa. 15: 24–30. Though he seemed outwardly to have lost everything, in what was he still able to rejoice?

2 In what assurance about the future was David able to rest? Have you any similar confidence?

☐ **STUDY 50 Psalms 64 and 65**

Ps. 64, like 58 and 59, has for its theme the certainty of God's judgment upon the wicked. Ps. 65, on the other hand, is a psalm of praise to God, as the God of the whole earth, the only Saviour from sin, and the Giver of fruitful harvests.

1 Ps. 64. How are the psalmist's enemies described (verses 1–6)? What are the purpose and result of God's judgment? What truths should we take to heart, and act on when in similar circumstances?

2   Ps. 65. In verse 1, the psalmist says that praise is due to God. In the remaining verses, what can you find which moves you to praise God for all He is, and has done? Are the experiences mentioned in verses 3 and 4 known to you?

☐   **STUDY 51   Psalms 66 and 67**

Ps. 66 is a summons to the nations to join in praise to God for a great deliverance which He has wrought for His people, such as the deliverance of Jerusalem from Sennacherib. If this was the occasion, the speaker in verses 13–20 may well be King Hezekiah himself, speaking as the representative of the nation. Ps. 67 may belong to the same time. See Is. 37.

1   Ps. 66. Note in detail what God is here said to do with and for His people. What response ought this to move me to make? What is the condition of sharing in such an experience?

2   Ps. 67. Do we share the longing of the psalmist that all nations might know God and His salvation? By what means did he think it would be achieved? *Cf.* Mt. 5: 14–16; 1 Pet. 2: 9, 10.

☐   **STUDY 52   Psalm 68: 1–18**

This psalm describes the onward march of God through history to His final triumph. The threefold reference to the sanctuary in verses 17, 24, 35 suggests that, like Ps. 24, it was written to celebrate the bringing of the ark to Jerusalem. See 2 Sa. 6: 15, 17, 18.

1   What effect does the appearing of God have on (a) His enemies (verses 1, 2), (b) the righteous (verses 3, 4), and (c) those in need (verses 5, 6)?

2   In the historical retrospect of verses 7–18, what aspects of God's character are revealed?

Notes
1   Verse 7. *Cf.* Jdg. 5: 4, 5.
2   Verses 13b, 14. The meaning is uncertain. Verse 13b may mention an item of spoil: see verse 12 and *cf.* Jdg. 5: 30. Or it may describe a symbol—like the golden wings of the cherubim (see Ex. 25: 20–22)—of a theophany. Verse 14 may be a picture of the kings and their armies fleeing as snow-flakes driven before a storm.
3   Verses 17, 18. God enters Zion with His heavenly hosts. *Cf.* Eph. 4: 8; Ps. 24: 7–10.

☐   **STUDY 53   Psalm 68: 19–35**

1   Verses 19–27. How is the blessedness of God's people described? In your own experience do you know God as He is here set forth? What may we also learn from these verses concerning the character and place of public worship?

2   Verses 28–35. What God has done (verses 7–18) and is doing (verses 19–27) is but the prelude to greater triumphs. What vision does the psalmist see of a world-wide homage paid to God, and how is this confirmed by other scriptures?

Note. Verse 30. 'The beasts that dwell among the reeds' represent Egypt; and the 'bulls' followed by their 'calves', other kings and their peoples.

☐   **STUDY 54   Psalm 69**

This psalm is notable, first because the New Testament quotes from it several times, and second, because amidst prayers of humble supplication, the psalmist suddenly breaks into cries of passionate imprecation (verses 22–28).

1   What is the cause of the psalmist's troubles? What is the chief concern of his prayer, and what does he expect will happen in the end?

2   What features in the psalmist's sufferings most closely prefigure those of our Lord, helping us to understand how deeply He tasted of human woe? *Cf.* Heb. 4: 15. Verses 20, 21 take us specially to Gethsemane and the cross; but at the point of deepest suffering, where the psalmist breaks out in imprecatory prayer, what did our Lord pray? See Lk. 23: 34.

3   In what respects do verses 22–28 foreshadow the judgment that has fallen upon the Jewish people? *Cf.* verses 22, 23 with Mt. 13: 14; Rom. 11: 9, 10; and verse 25 with Mt. 23: 38.

☐   **STUDY 55   Psalms 70 and 71**

These psalms are both reminiscent of other psalms. Ps. 70 is taken bodily from Ps. 40. Ps. 71: 1–3 is taken from Ps. 31: 1–3; and the rest of Ps. 71 is largely made up of fragments also found in other psalms.

1   What does the psalmist expect God to be to him, and to do for him, and what will such things make him do? Do you make similar confessions to God when you pray?

2   Observe the triple movement in Ps. 71: (a) faith, praying, rises to hope and praise (verses 1–8); (b) faith, under a renewed sense of urgent need, falls back into prayer, and again rises to hope and praise (verse 9–16); (c) faith, for the third time driven to prayer, rises quickly to assurance, praise and witness, and there abides (verses 20, 22–24). What does this teach us concerning continuance in prayer?

☐   **STUDY 56   Psalm 72**

This is a prophetic psalm, in which Christ is typified by Solomon, whose name means 'peace'.

1   What are the two outstanding personal characteristics of Christ as King, as seen in this psalm? See verses 1, 2 and 12–14; and *cf.* Ps. 116: 5. What does the psalm say will be (a) the results of His rule (verses 3–7, 12–14, 16, 17), and (b) the extent of His rule (verses 8–11)?

2   Does not this psalm give a perfect picture of that happy earth which men are vainly trying to bring into being by their own wisdom and work? But, according to Scripture, who alone can bring it to pass, and to whom therefore should men look for its accomplishment? See verses 1, 17–19; and *cf.* Acts 4: 12; Eph. 1: 3.

Notes
1   Verse 8. The 'River' is the Euphrates.
2   Verses 18, 19. This doxology is not part of the original psalm, but is added as the close of Book 2.

For Studies 57–70 on the Psalms see p. 379.

---

1 KINGS

Introduction

1 and 2 Kings form a single unit, the present somewhat arbitrary division having originated in the Vulgate. They give an account and complete history of the kings and the kingdoms ('of the king-doms' is the probable literal rendering of the titles). The account bears marks of being the work of a single author using as his sources various documents (see 1 Ki. 11: 41; 14: 19, 29; 15: 7, *etc.*) including prophetic memoirs. It is important to remember that the whole is written from the religious and prophetic point of view, not from that of the secular historian. As *The New Bible Commentary* remarks: 'This is the explanation why certain of the kings who were most important for their contemporaries, *e.g.*, Omri (1 Ki. xvi. 23–28), Azariah or Uzziah (2 Ki. xv. 1–7), Jeroboam II (2 Ki. xiv. 23–29), are passed over in virtual silence. It is spiritual, not political lessons,

that we are to learn. That is why the two periods of crisis, the reigns of Ahab for the north and of Hezekiah for the south, are given at special length.'

Expressed concisely, the theme of the book is that of Israel as the redeemed people of Jehovah, bearing His Name, and the kings as His representatives. Thus a wicked king is a paradox, as well as historically evil, and a good king by righteous acts is setting forth the rule of God. The sin of the people inevitably leads to the captivities, and throughout, political incidents are shown to be the effect of the fidelity or idolatry of the people. One proof of this is that prophetic activity is prominent in the reigns of wicked kings.

Analysis

1 – 11	The last days of the united kingdom.	
	1: 1 – 2: 11	David's last days and charge to Solomon.
	2: 12 – 4: 34	Solomon, his character and wisdom.
	5 – 8	The Temple.
	9 – 11	Solomon's magnificence and failure.
12 – 16	The division, and the divided kingdoms to the accession of Ahab.	
17 – 22	Elijah.	

☐ **STUDY 1   1 Kings 1**

1   Get hold of the story. Who supported Adonijah, and who supported Solomon, and by what means was Adonijah's attempt to seize the throne frustrated? What may we learn about the character of each of these men?

2   This is the last mention of Nathan in Scripture. In his actions here and also in 2 Sa. 7 and 12 how does he exemplify by his faithful and disinterested conduct our duty as servants of God?

Notes
1   Verse 5. Adonijah, as David's eldest surviving son (see 2 Sa. 3: 4), had a claim to recognition (see 1 Ki. 2: 15). At the same time this might be overruled by the king (verses 20 and 27).
2   Verses 52, 53. Solomon spares Adonijah on certain conditions, but commands him to withdraw from public affairs.

☐ **STUDY 2   1 Kings 2**

1   Enumerate the points David made in his final advice to his son Solomon.

2   How and why were Adonijah, Joab, and Shimei put to death? Solomon's own reaction was to let bygones be bygones, but David counselled against this, and Solomon acted accordingly. What do

you think was David's motive in giving the counsel he did? What lessons may we learn from Adonijah's life-story?

☐ **STUDY 3   1 Kings 3 and 4**

1   Solomon's request was pleasing to God (3: 10), but was it the highest gift he could have asked? *Cf.* Ex. 33: 13; Phil. 3: 8, 10. What do you put first in prayer? What do we learn of God's dealings with man from the way in which He answered Solomon's request?

2   What good things are said about Solomon in these two chapters, and what benefits did his rule bring to his people? What, according to the writer, was the deepest ground of his prosperity?

Note. 4: 4b. This was true only at the very beginning of Solomon's reign. See 2: 35.

☐ **STUDY 4   1 Kings 5**

1   To what great task did Solomon first set his hand, and what motives moved him to undertake it? Are we as ready to speak to a non-Christian friend of the goodness of God and of our desire to serve Him, as Solomon was to speak to Hiram?

2   What may we learn from the fact that even in the arrangements which Solomon made with Hiram for materials and skilled labour, he acted according to the wisdom given him by God? *Cf.* Eph. 5: 15–17; Jas. 1: 5; 3: 17.

☐ **STUDY 5   1 Kings 6: 1 – 7: 12**

1   Try to form a mental picture of 'the house of the Lord'. What was its length, its breadth, its height? What the size of the porch, and what of the most holy place, here called 'the inner sanctuary' (RSV) or 'the oracle' (AV)? Notice, too, the side rooms, arranged in three storeys round the sides and back of the house. These would take away from the narrow appearance of the building, and provide space for storage, *etc.* It may help you to draw a sketch, keeping to scale (a cubit was about eighteen inches). Draw in also the five buildings in the outer court (7: 1–12).

2   Of what material were the walls made, with what were they lined on the inner side, and how adorned? Observe also the care expended upon the design and workmanship of the two sets of doors. What may we learn from these things? *Cf.* 1 Ch. 22: 5, 14–16; 1 Cor. 3: 12–15.

Note. 7: 2. 'The House of the Forest of Lebanon': so called because of the number of pillars made from the cedars of Lebanon. It was a Hall of Assembly.

☐ STUDY 6   1 Kings 7: 13 – 8: 11

Today's portion describes (a) the making of the brass (or bronze) furnishings and implements for the Temple court, 7: 13–47; (b) the golden furniture and utensils for the house itself, 7: 48–50. Many of the details are difficult to grasp, but it is possible to distinguish the two great pillars, with their ornamental capitals, the great basin resting upon twelve oxen, and the ten carriages with wheels, richly ornamental, and carrying lavers; and also within the house the golden altar of incense, the table of shew bread, and ten candlesticks or lampstands. There was also a brass altar in the Temple court, which is mentioned later (see 8: 64).

1   What may we learn concerning our own service for Christ from the spirit and aim that animated Solomon (*cf.* 2 Cor. 9: 7; Rom. 12: 11), and from the fact that he pursued the task through seven years until it was finished (*cf.* Acts 14: 26; 20: 24; 2 Tim. 4: 7; Lk. 14: 28, 29)?

2   Finally, when all was prepared, the ark was brought in to the place reserved for it under the wings of the cherubim in the most holy place. Is the Lord Christ thus enthroned in you, His temple? *Cf.* Eph. 3: 16, 17. In what ways is His indwelling manifested in your life?

☐ STUDY 7   1 Kings 8: 12–66

1   Verses 14–21. What promise is here spoken of as having been fulfilled? Are there experiences in your life of which you can say 'God . . . with his hand has fulfilled what he promised with his mouth'? Observe how, in verses 22–53, thanksgiving for the fulfilment of the promise stimulated further prayer. What seven particular petitions did Solomon make, and on what grounds did he base his prayer?

2   Verses 54–62. In this 'blessing' how did Solomon sum up Israel's story? What two petitions did he offer, and to what ends, and what charge did he give the people? Consider how applicable his words are to ourselves.

Notes
1   Verse 12. 'Thick darkness': there was no light in the most holy place, to symbolize the inscrutable mystery of the divine nature. The ark symbolized His presence in the midst of His people.
2   Verse 16. 'My name': a phrase used frequently in this chapter as signifying God in the fullness of His self-revelation.
3   Verse 51. 'Iron furnace': *i.e.*, one in which iron is smelted.
4   Verse 65. 'Seven days' or 'seven days and seven days': *i.e.*, seven for the dedication of the altar, and seven for the feast, as explained in 2 Ch. 7: 8, 9.

☐ STUDY 8   1 Kings 9: 1 – 10: 13

1   Comparing 9: 3 carefully with 8: 29, in what two respects did God exceed Solomon's request? Observe also the close relation between God's promise and His commands, and between His fulfilment of His promise and man's obedience. *Cf.* Jn. 14: 14, 15, 21; 15: 7; 1 Jn. 3: 22. What do we see in today's passage of the fulfilment to Solomon of God's promise in 3: 12, 13?

2   In what ways is the Queen of Sheba an example to us? Consider the purpose of her visit, the difficulties of it, and her reward.

Notes
1   9: 14. A talent of gold, it is reckoned, would be the equivalent of £6,150, but would in those days have a far higher purchasing power.
2   9: 25. *Cf.* 2 Ch. 8: 13, 14.

☐ STUDY 9   1 Kings 10: 14 – 11: 43

1   Solomon was outwardly at the height of his power, wealth and fame (see 10: 14–29). But what was going on within his heart in respect (a) of his affections, and (b) of his relation to God (see 11: 1–8)? Read Pr. 4: 23–27. What was God's chief charge against him?

2   How does the account of the events of 11: 14–40 bring out God's overruling hand? *Cf.* Dn. 4: 34, 35; Ps. 135: 5, 6. What effect should this truth have upon a believing heart? *Cf.* Acts 4: 23–30.

☐ STUDY 10   1 Kings 12: 1–32

1   Study the characters of the two kings, Rehoboam and Jeroboam. To what factors would you attribute the division of the kingdom?

2   What four actions of Jeroboam are spoken of in verses 25–32, and what was their purpose? Clever as they were politically and according to human judgment, wherein lay their fatal error? See verse 30; 13: 33, 34; 2 Ki. 17: 21.

☐ STUDY 11   1 Kings 12: 33 – 13: 34

1   What was the root fault in Jeroboam's character, and how did God in His mercy seek to show him the folly of the course he was pursuing? See 12: 33 – 13: 10.

2   What punishment fell upon 'the man of God . . . out of Judah' and why? *Cf.* 20: 36, and contrast our Lord's firmness in Mt. 16: 22, 23.

STUDY 12   1 Kings 14

1   Jeroboam and Ahijah had both been called of God, the one to be king (11: 31), and the other as prophet. What was the difference between them in their carrying out of their office, and how does this show what qualities are required in a servant of God?

2   What two pictures of Rehoboam's reign are given in verses 21–31? What light do they throw upon the state of the kingdom of Judah, and upon Rehoboam's character?

Notes
1   The name Abijah, given by Jeroboam to his son, shows that Jeroboam still worshipped Jehovah, for Abijah means 'my father is Jah'.
2   Verse 17. 'Tirzah' was the residence of the kings of the northern kingdom. *Cf.* 15: 21; 16: 15.
3   Verses 23, 24. All that is mentioned in these verses was associated with idolatry. *Cf.* Je. 2: 20.

STUDY 13   1 Kings 15: 1 – 16: 7

1   In this portion two kings of Judah are mentioned and two of Israel. Who were they? What facts do we learn about each of them?

2   What is the one standard by which these men are judged in Scripture? In relation to this standard, which of them were disapproved, and why? And which of them was approved, and why? What does this teach us concerning eternal values?

Notes
1   15: 10. 'His mother's name': strictly his grandmother (see verses 2 and 8). Maachah apparently continued to be officially 'queen mother' (see verse 13).
2   15: 17. 'Ramah' was only five miles from Jerusalem to the north.
3   16: 7. 'Because he destroyed it': *cf.* 15: 27, 29.

STUDY 14   1 Kings 16: 8–34

1   In the northern kingdom the dynasties of Jeroboam and Baasha were utterly destroyed, as later was that of Omri (see 21: 22). How does the story of this kingdom show that the people departed farther and farther from God until the climax was reached with Omri (verse 25) and Ahab (verse 30)? What may this teach us as to the self-propagating power of sin? Yet in Judah the royal line of David continued. Why this difference? Consider what is said in 11: 36 and 15: 4.

2   What was the special sin of Ahab, by which he provoked the Lord to anger? How did he go beyond what previous kings of Israel had done, and what led him to do it?

Notes

1 Verse 24. Omri was an able and powerful ruler, whose name is mentioned in the ancient Assyrian records and in the Moabite stone of Mesha. His selection of Samaria as the capital was an important event in Israel's history.

2 Verses 31, 32. The calves set up by Jeroboam (see 12: 28) were supposed to represent the God of Israel. Ahab's sin was greater in that he worshipped Baal, the god of Tyre, and built in Samaria a 'house of Baal'.

☐ **STUDY 15 1 Kings 17 and 18**

1 How was the prophet trained in faith and obedience for the supreme struggle on Mount Carmel? What did the experiences at the brook Cherith and in Zarephath teach him? What was the supreme issue at stake between him and King Ahab?

2 What was the secret of Elijah's strength and victory? See 18: 41–45; Jas. 5: 17, 18, and *cf.* 17: 1 with Heb. 11: 27b.

Note. 18: 45, 46. 'To Jezreel': about seventeen or eighteen miles. This extraordinary feat of endurance indicates that the prophet was keyed up to a high degree of nervous tension.

☐ **STUDY 16 1 Kings 19**

Prophets among the people of Israel were held in high regard. Elijah therefore supposed that after so great a moral victory as that won on Mount Carmel, king and nation would return to Jehovah. But Jezebel had no such awe in her heart, and Elijah found himself faced by her wrathful fury. It was a rude shock to all his hopes.

1 What difference do you notice between the account of Elijah's flight at this time and that of his previous flights to Cherith and Zarephath? What causes for his deep depression and sense of failure can you think of? Read the story of verses 4–18 in the light of Ps. 103: 13, 14. How did God comfort, teach and restore Elijah?

2 When God's call came to Elisha, how did he respond? Are you thus ready to do God's will, in whatever sphere of service He may appoint? *Cf.* Mk. 1: 15–20. What do we learn from this passage about the way God plans for His work to be begun by one of His servants and carried on by another? *Cf.* 1 Cor. 3: 6.

Notes

1 Verse 8. 'To Horeb the mount of God': the site of God's covenant with Israel (see Dt. 4: 9–20). This was probably the object of Elijah's journey from the first.

2 Verse 19. 'Twelve yoke of oxen' indicates a wealthy farm.

☐ **STUDY 17 1 Kings 20**

The reappearance of true prophets of Jehovah in this chapter is striking. It seems to indicate that Elijah's ministry had effected a change in the whole attitude of public opinion, and even in Ahab himself.

1 What was the difference between Ben-hadad's two demands which made Ahab reject the second, though he had yielded to the first? What threat did Ben-hadad make, and what was Ahab's answer?

2 How many times in this chapter is the intervention of a prophet recorded? What may we ourselves learn from the messages these men were sent of God to deliver?

☐ **STUDY 18   1 Kings 21**

1 Consider the parts played by Ahab, Jezebel, and the elders of Jezreel respectively in the murder of Naboth. What was the special guilt of each? What was it that distinguished Elijah from all these? What do we learn from his example of the qualities God wants in us if He is to do His work?

2 Sum up what you have learnt of Ahab's character from chapters 20 and 21.

Notes
1 Verses 2 and 3. Ahab's offer was fair in itself, but when he failed to gain his desire he was displeased. Yet Naboth, according to the law, had the right to refuse. See Nu. 36: 7.
2 Verse 15. We learn from 2 Ki. 9: 26 that Naboth's sons were also put to death, that there might be no surviving heir.

☐ **STUDY 19   1 Kings 22**

1 Compare the attitude of the two kings in regard to asking counsel of the Lord. Did they not both err: Ahab because he would not have done it at all but for Jehoshaphat, and Jehoshaphat because he did it *after* the decision was made? Do we sometimes find ourselves committing both these errors?

2 What may we learn from Ahab's foolish hatred of Micaiah? What was the reason for it, and to what end did it lead? *Cf.* Jn. 8: 40. Are we ever guilty of asking advice only from people who will tell us what we want to hear?

Notes
1 Verse 3. 'Ramoth-gilead': possibly one of the towns mentioned in 20: 34.
2 Verse 6. These prophets were probably prophets of the calf-worship which Jeroboam had established (12: 28, 29). In name they may have been prophets of Jehovah, God of Israel, but they were not true prophets as Micaiah was.
3 Verse 31. An ungrateful return for Ahab's clemency; see 20: 31–34. It underlines the truth of the unknown prophet's prediction in 20: 42.

JOHN 1 - 12

Introduction

The author of this Gospel claims to have been an eye-witness of the scenes that he records (1: 14; 19: 35; *cf.* 1 Jn. 1: 1–3), and in 21: 24 his identity with 'the disciple whom Jesus loved' is asserted. Among the many reasons for identifying this disciple with John the son of Zebedee, one of the most striking is the Evangelist's habit of referring to the Baptist as 'John' only, and never mentioning the son of Zebedee by name.

The other three Gospels are chiefly concerned with our Lord's ministry in Galilee; a bare hint is all that they give us that He so much as visited Jerusalem between His baptism and the final Passover (Mt. 23: 37; Lk. 13: 34; and Lk. 4: 44). John, on the other hand, has little to say about our Lord's work in Galilee (2: 1–12; 4: 43–54; 6); for the most part the scene of his narrative is Judaea, and especially Jerusalem, where almost from the first the Lord was rejected (1: 11; 4: 43, 44; 5; *etc.*).

It is important to observe that in the record of Jesus' ministry up to His death, seven miracles are recorded in this Gospel. These are (1) the turning of water into wine (2: 1–11); (2) the healing of the nobleman's son (4: 46–54); (3) the healing of the impotent man (5: 2–9); (4) the feeding of the five thousand (6: 4–13); (5) the walking on the water (6: 16–21); (6) the healing of the man born blind (9: 1–7); (7) the raising of Lazarus from the dead (11: 1–44). John calls these miracles 'signs', by which he means that they have a meaning beyond themselves, and point to the identity of Jesus as the Christ, and to His corresponding works in the spiritual realm, such as the raising of the spiritually dead, the opening of the eyes of the spiritually blind, *etc.*

The purpose of the Gospel, and particularly of the signs recorded in it, is clearly stated, 'that you may believe that Jesus is the Christ, the Son of God, and that believing you may have life in his name' (20: 31). It shows the divine Word coming to His own people, revealing the Father to them both by teaching and by 'signs', and yet rejected and persecuted to the death. To the world this Gospel reveals the tremendous claims of the Lord Jesus and the awfulness of rejecting Him. To the disciple it reveals the implications of accepting Him, showing the interdependence of love and obedience, of life and feeding upon the Lord, of fruit-bearing and abiding in Him.

The section 7: 53 – 8: 11 is omitted by all the oldest Greek manuscripts now existing, with one exception, and its style and vocabulary are more like those of Luke (in whose Gospel four manuscripts insert it) than those of John. But though this section was probably not written by John, it bears every evidence of truth, and we may thankfully accept it as part of the inspired Word of God.

Analysis

1: 1–18	The Preface or Prologue. The eternal, divine Word became flesh and dwelt among us.
1: 19 – 12: 50	Jesus reveals Himself to the world.
	1: 19–51 By the testimony of the Baptist and the first disciples.
	2 – 4 By signs and teaching among Jews, Samaritans and Galilaeans.
	5 The healing of the paralytic in Jerusalem begins the conflict between Jesus and the Jews.
	6 Jesus is revealed as the sustainer of life.
	7: 1–52 Jesus at the Feast of Tabernacles; the people divided; vain attempt to arrest Him.
	7: 53 – 8: 11 The woman taken in adultery.
	8: 12–59 Jesus is the light of the world, and the I AM.
	9 Blindness cured, and blindness intensified.
	10 Jesus is the Good Shepherd, and He is One with the Father.
	11 Jesus is the resurrection and the life.
	12 Jesus is about to be glorified through death. Summary of the effects of His ministry.
13 – 17	Jesus reveals Himself to His disciples in the farewell discourse and the High-Priestly prayer.
18 – 21	Jesus is glorified in His arrest, His trial, His passion and His resurrection.

☐ **STUDY 1   John 1: 1–18**

1   Why is Jesus here called 'the Word'? What is His relation to God; to the world; to men? See the whole passage.

2   Who does not, and who does become a child of God? By what means is one brought into this new status?

3   Note all the allusions to 'light' and associated ideas (*e.g.*, 'glory') in this passage. How much of the purpose of Jesus' coming does this explain?

Note. Verse 16. 'Grace upon grace': *i.e.*, one grace succeeding another.

☐ **STUDY 2   John 1: 19–34**

1   What do we learn here about (a) the character, (b) the work, of John the Baptist? See also verses 6–8 and 3: 28–30.

2   Verses 26–34. What testimony does John the Baptist here bear to Jesus? How much of this did John learn about Him through his experience at Christ's baptism? Do these truths mean something to you?

Note. Verse 29. 'He saw Jesus coming': probably after the forty days in the wilderness, when He was tempted by Satan. That Jesus' baptism had already taken place is shown by verse 32. *Cf.* Lk. 3: 21, 22.

☐ **STUDY 3   John 1: 35–51**

1   Describe what it was that brought each of these five men to Jesus. How far did they understand who Jesus was? What account of Him can *you* give to others?

2   Verses 48, 49. Why did Jesus' answer elicit the response of Nathanael? See 2: 25. What do verses 47–50 reveal of Nathanael's character?

Notes
1   Verse 42. Cephas = Peter = Rock.
2   Verses 47, 51. An allusion to the story of Jacob in Gn. 32: 24–29 and 28: 12, 13.
3   Verse 51. This word, as shown by the plural 'you', was spoken not about Nathanael only, but about all the disciples. Jesus would be revealed to them as the true and final Mediator between God and man.

☐ **STUDY 4   John 2: 1–22**

1   Verses 1–11 present the first of the seven 'signs' (see Introduction), which reveal the identity of Jesus and stimulate faith (verse 11). What particular aspect of Jesus' glory does this miracle display?

What change in our life does turning the water into wine represent? Cf. 2 Cor. 5: 17. What can we learn from Mary's response to Jesus?

2   The idea of the 'Temple' unites verses 13–17 with 18–22. How does Jesus appear in each incident? By what authority does He drive out the traders? Cf. Mal. 3: 1–3. What crisis does this incident foreshadow in the mind of Jesus? What did He foresee concerning the cost and character of His mission?

Notes
1   Verse 4. The English, even in RSV, makes Jesus' words seem disrespectful, but in the Greek the form of address is perfectly courteous. Jesus makes it clear that He depends upon no human instructions, even from His mother, but only upon that which God appoints. He is awaiting His Father's instructions.
2   Verses 14–16. See *TNTC* (p. 61) for discussion whether there were two cleansings of the Temple, one at the beginning of Jesus' ministry, as here, and one at the end, as recorded in the Synoptics.

☐   **STUDY 5   John 2: 23 – 3: 21**

1   Why was Jesus not satisfied with the faith spoken of in 2: 23? Cf. 4: 48; 6: 26, 30; Mt. 13: 14. Is my faith the kind that pleases God?

2   What was right and what was lacking in Nicodemus' assessment of Jesus? How did Jesus' answer correct him? What is involved in being 'born of the Spirit', and why is it needed? Cf. Mt. 18: 3; Jn. 1: 12, 13; 2 Cor. 5: 17; Rom. 8: 8, 9.

3   Why was the lifting up of the Son of man necessary? (Note 'must' in verse 15.) On what ground are men judged and condemned? Where do you stand in relation to these truths?

Notes
1   Verse 5. 'Born of water' probably refers to John's baptism.
2   Verse 8. As with the wind, so with the movement of the Spirit, the effect is real and recognizable, although the process is hidden.
3   Verses 12, 13. The gospel speaks of heavenly things, of which Christ is the sole revealer. Cf. 3: 31, 32; Mt. 11: 27.

☐   **STUDY 6   John 3: 22–36**

1   How might one have expected John to have replied to the statement of verse 26? Consider the quality of character and the principles brought out in his answer. How far do you share his attitude to Christ? How does it apply to your situation?

2   What is said about Jesus in verses 31, 32, 34, 35, which set Him apart from and above all others?

3 'Receives his testimony', 'believes in the Son', 'does not obey the Son' (verses 33, 36). What kinds of response to Jesus Christ do these phrases describe? To what consequences do they lead?

Notes
1 Verse 32. 'No one': *i.e.*, generally speaking; it is qualified in verse 33.
2 Verse 33. 'Sets his seal': he both confirms his acceptance of the truth of God's word and in his consequent experience proves the truth of it. *Cf.* 7: 17.

☐ **STUDY 7 John 4: 1–26**

1 What did our Lord mean by 'living water' (verse 10)? Why, when He had wakened in the woman a desire for it, did He not at once grant her request? What was necessary before He could do so?

2 Trace the successive steps by which Jesus brought the woman to feel her need of salvation, and pointed her to Himself. What can we learn from this to help us as we seek to lead others to Him?

3 In verses 19, 20 was the woman evading the demand for a personal response? How does Jesus' answer meet the need of those today who evade the claims of God by professing to follow a correct form of worship? Where must all look for salvation?

Note. Verse 20. 'This mountain': *i.e.*, Mount Gerizim, where the Samaritans had built a temple. The temple had been destroyed, but the Samaritans regarded the place as holy.

☐ **STUDY 8 John 4: 27–54**

1 How do the previous verses explain and verses 35–38 develop the truth which Jesus expressed in verse 34? What gives you most satisfaction in life?

2 Two groups of Samaritans and the Capernaum official all believed in Jesus, but through different means. What was the particular truth about Him which brought each of them to faith? To what did 'the second sign' (verse 54) point? What aspect of the Lord's character or power led you to Him?

3 Verse 48 seems to be a test of the man's sincerity. How would you explain Jesus' words here?

Note. Verses 35–38. In the natural world there were yet four months until harvest, but in the spiritual sphere in this instance reaping was possible at once. Someone else had done the sowing.

☐ **STUDY 9 John 5: 1–29**

1 Verses 2–9, the third 'sign'. What features of Jesus' power does it reveal? What did He do for the man, and demand from the man, apart from making him walk? See verses 6 and 14.

2 Verses 17–29. In what terms is Jesus' relationship with God described? What functions concerning judgment has God given to Jesus, and why? How do these truths concern us?

3 Verses 16–18. What connection has Jesus' statement in verse 17 with His healing on the sabbath? How does this agree with Gn. 2: 2, 3, and how does it answer the Jews' criticism of His action?

Note. Verse 25. What is meant here is spiritual resurrection from the death of sin. Contrast verses 28, 29.

☐ **STUDY 10 John 5: 30–47**

1 To what four different testimonies to Himself does Jesus appeal? Which does He Himself regard as of least importance, and why? Contrast 8: 14.

2 Verses 39, 40. Is it still possible to study the Bible without finding life? If so, what is lacking? What reasons does Jesus give for the Jews' failure? Cf. 2 Cor. 3: 14–16.

Note. Verse 31. 'Not true': in the sense of not being accepted as true. Cf. Dt. 19: 15; Mt. 18: 16; Jn. 8: 13, 14.

☐ **STUDY 11 John 6: 1–21**

1 Taking this fourth 'sign' in the context of verses 1–13, note what it reveals concerning (a) why the people were attracted to Jesus; (b) His own attitude to the people; (c) His testing of His disciples' faith; (d) His use of their co-operation; (e) the source of the answer to men's need. What over-all lesson was this miracle intended to convey?

2 Verse 15. Why did not Jesus wish to be made king by these people? What may we learn from His withdrawing from the place of success to be by Himself? Cf. Lk. 5: 15, 16.

Notes
1 Verse 7. A denarius may be valued as a day's wage for a labourer; cf. Mt. 20: 2.
2 Verse 14. 'The prophet who is to come': cf. Dt. 18: 15; Mt. 11: 3; He is here identified by the people with the Messiah, as verse 15 shows.

☐ **STUDY 12 John 6: 22–40**

The miracle of verses 4–13 is the basis of the dialogue between Jesus and the Jews in verses 25–59.

1 The people saw the outward form of the miracle, but failed to discern what it signified spiritually (verse 26). Why? From what

motives did they seek Jesus? Are you more concerned about spiritual development than material prosperity (verse 27)?

2 'Labour' in verse 27 is literally 'work for'. How did the people relate this word (a) to the work they were expected to do (verse 28), (b) to the work of Moses compared with Jesus (verses 30, 31)? What work did Jesus (a) require from them (verse 29) and (b) offer from Himself (verse 32–40)? What, therefore, is the answer to the question in verse 28?

3 How do verses 35–40 present God's answer to man's hunger?

Note. Verses 22–25 explain the astonishment of the crowd at finding Jesus next day on the Capernaum side of the lake. They had noticed that He had not gone with the disciples.

☐ **STUDY 13   John 6: 41–71**

Today's portion falls into four parts: (a) verses 41–51, Jesus' reply to murmurings of the Jews; (b) verses 52–59, Jesus' answers to the wranglings of the Jews; (c) verses 60–65, Jesus' reply to murmurings of His disciples; (d) verses 66–71, Jesus asks the Twelve, 'Will you also go away?'

1 Comparing verses 36, 37 with 43–45, why do you think some people will not accept Jesus' words? By what steps do others come to experience salvation?

2 The closing verses 60–71 make clear that what Jesus offers to men is not fleshly or material gain (*cf.* verse 27), but spiritual life through union with Himself. What three reasons does Peter give why he and his fellow disciples remained faithful when many others went back?

3 How did Jesus give His flesh for the life of the world? What is meant by eating His flesh and drinking His blood?

Notes
1 Verse 62. The return of the Son of man to heaven (*cf.* 3 : 13) will be a greater wonder than the words just spoken. It will confirm the divine character of Jesus and of His words.
2 The approaching Passover Feast was clearly in our Lord's thought as He spoke, and there may be anticipating allusions to the Lord's Supper; but Jesus is speaking in this discourse, not of the sacrament itself, but of the truths of which the sacrament is only one expression. Note the manner of true participation (verses 35, 63, 68, 69).

☐ **STUDY 14   John 7: 1–24**

Chapters 7: 1 – 10: 21 give an account of Jesus' visit to Jerusalem at the Feast of Tabernacles six months before His death. The story vividly portrays the various attitudes towards Jesus among different groups. These groups fall into two main classes: one, 'the Jews', who included the chief priests,

Pharisees, rulers and 'the people of Jerusalem', and the other, 'the people', that is, the general multitude from all parts, who were attending the feast. The first of these two classes was, in the main, hostile to Jesus.

1 How do the words of Jesus' brothers in verses 3–8 show that they did not understand Him? What did Jesus mean by 'my time'? The world's attitude to Jesus prevented Him from showing Himself to them, as other men might (verses 4, 7). Can *you* expect any different reception from the world (*cf.* 15: 18–21)? Has verse 13 any reproach for you?

2 Verses 17, 18. What two tests does our Lord suggest by which a man can discover whether Jesus' teaching was true and of divine origin? What will it cost you to apply these tests?

Notes
1 Verses 8, 10. Jesus did not break His word. He meant that He was not going up to the feast just then, and at their direction.
2 Verses 21–24. The law of Moses commanded circumcision on the eighth day after birth (Gn. 17: 12; Lv. 12: 3), and it was the practice of the Jews to perform the rite on that day, *even if it fell upon the sabbath*. Jesus argued that to make a man's whole body well on the sabbath had even more justification than to circumcise him.

☐ **STUDY 15 John 7: 25-52**

1 What illustrations are found in these verses (a) of the deep impression made by the Lord Jesus upon many; and yet (b) how their incipient faith was checked by ignorance (verses 27–29), or prejudice (verses 35, 36), or pride (verses 48–52)? Is one of these hindering me?

2 The chief priests and the Pharisees by no means saw eye to eye in most matters, but they were united against Jesus. What action did they take at this time, and what prevented its success? It is often said, 'No thinking person now believes that . . .'. What example of this attitude can you find in this passage?

3 In what way is the promise of verses 37, 38 an advance on that of 4: 13, 14? What difference does the Holy Spirit make to your life? *Cf.* Acts 1: 8.

Note. Verse 39. The Spirit was already present and active in the world, but the particular promise of Joel 2: 28 was not fulfilled until the ascended and enthroned Christ gave the Holy Spirit on the Day of Pentecost. See Acts 2: 16–18, 33.

☐ **STUDY 16 John 7: 53 – 8: 29**

1 For the passage 7: 53 – 8: 11, see Introduction. It has perhaps been introduced here as an illustration of 8: 15. What two different types of sinner can you see in the Pharisees and in the woman? Why

did Jesus treat her so gently? Would His words to her bring conviction of her sin?

2   In verses 13–29 what does Jesus say about His origin, His ultimate destination, His relation to the world, His relation to God?

3   What was lacking in the Pharisees which prevented them from recognizing the truth of Jesus' words? How can I see the light of truth? How does light lead to life? See verses 12, 24.

Notes
1   8: 12. An allusion to the pillar of fire which guided the Israelites on their journey through the wilderness (see Nu. 9: 15–23), and which was commemorated during the Feast of Tabernacles by brilliant lighting of the Temple.
2   Verses 13, 14. There is no contradiction with 5: 31. There Jesus says that if He had been the sole witness in His own cause, His witness would not have been true. But in both passages He goes on to point out that He is not alone in His witness. See verses 17, 18.

☐ **STUDY 17   John 8: 30–59**

1   The form of expression in Greek in verse 31 shows that 'the Jews' here did not commit themselves to Jesus as much as the 'many' in verse 30. What steps leading to full freedom are seen in verses 31–36? What is this freedom? In what sense did the Jews claim to be free? Are you truly free?

2   This section is concerned with the real meaning of parentage. For what reasons did Jesus argue that these Jews were not truly the children of Abraham or of God, but of the devil? What evidence did Jesus give that He is God's Son? Why were they not able to see this?

Notes
1   Verse 51. 'He will never see death': *i.e.*, know the experience of that death which is God's judgment on sin; *cf.* Gn. 2: 17; Jn. 5: 24; 11: 26.
2   Verse 56. 'My day': Abraham in faith saw ahead to the day of Christ's incarnation, and anticipated His saving work.
3   Verse 58. 'I am': the divine name, as in Ex. 3: 14.

☐ **STUDY 18   John 9**

1   This is the sixth of the seven 'signs'. To which aspect of Jesus' work does it point? See verses 5, 39. In how many ways is the opening of this man's eyes to be compared with the giving of spiritual sight? Does your personal experience of Jesus' power give you the same assurance in answering His critics as this man had?

2   Explain verses 39–41. Detail the ways in which the words and actions of the Pharisees in verses 13–34 illustrate this passage.

Note. Verse 14. The 'work' for which the Pharisees condemned Jesus as breaking the sabbath was making clay, as well as healing. The latter was allowed, but only in an emergency.

☐ **STUDY 19   John 10: 1–21**

Compare Je. 23: 1–4. By their attitude to the blind man of chapter 9 the Pharisees, who claimed to be the spiritual guides of Israel as the people of God, had shown themselves to be 'thieves and robbers' (verses 1, 8), like the false prophets of the Old Testament.

1   Verses 1–10. Why does Jesus call Himself 'the door of the sheep'? What are the privileges and blessings of those who enter in? How do the sheep recognize the true shepherd? What does he do to them? Do you know his voice?

2   What are the marks of the good shepherd? Can you find in verses 11–18 (a) proof that our Lord's death was not a mere martyrdom, (b) the purpose of His life and death, and (c) an incentive to missionary work? *Cf.* Rev. 7: 9, 10, 15–17.

Notes
1   Verse 3. 'Hear': *i.e.*, listen attentively to, and so obey.
2   Jesus is both 'door' and 'shepherd'. Others also are under-shepherds (Acts 20: 28, 29; 1 Pet. 5: 2–4) who must themselves first enter through the 'door'.

☐ **STUDY 20   John 10: 22–42**

1   Why would a plain answer to the Jews' question of verse 24 have been useless? What indications of the nature of Jesus' Person were already being given? See verses 25, 32, 37, 38. Why were the Jews incapable of seeing this? Do your works corroborate your words?

2   In the statements of verses 27, 28 how is the sheep's relation to the shepherd described, and how the shepherd's relation to the sheep? On what grounds given in verses 28, 29 can you be sure that you will never perish?

3   In what terms does Jesus describe His relationship with God, and what evidence does He give in support of His claim? How far are the words of the Jews at the end of verse 33 correct? What ought they to have done?

Notes
1   Verse 30. The word 'one' is neuter in the Greek: 'a unity', not 'one person'.
2   Verses 34–36. See Ps. 82: 6. Even the judges of Israel, acting as God's representatives, were called 'gods'. The Jews should have seen that Jesus was far superior to them. This comparison with the men of the Old Testament is sufficient argument to refute the charge of blasphemy. Jesus does not imply that He is merely a man like them.

☐ **STUDY 21   John 11: 1–27**

The seventh 'sign'.

1   Compare verse 4 with 9: 3. Explain the apparent contradiction both in verse 4 and also in verses 5, 6. See verses 14, 15. Can you see why God sometimes seems to delay answering your prayer?

2   What direction and assurance do verses 9, 10 give for the conduct of your life? *Cf.* 9: 4, 5.

3   In verses 21, 22, 24 Martha makes three correct but limited statements. In respect to each of them Jesus' answer in verses 25, 26 reveals that He has within Himself infinitely greater powers than she knew. What are they?

Note. Verse 26. 'Shall never die': for the believer death is no longer death. It introduces him into a new state of life. See Note on Jn. 8: 51.

☐ **STUDY 22   John 11: 28–44**

1   What is the special significance of this seventh 'sign'? How is it related to the events which Jesus was shortly to experience as the climax of His work? In what way was the glory of God revealed?

2   Why did Jesus pray aloud before calling Lazarus from the tomb? What does this teach about the means by which His miracles were accomplished? *Cf.* Jn. 5: 19, 20; 14: 10.

Note. Verses 33–38. The word 'weep' in verse 33 is the wailing of mourners; that in verse 35 implies silent tears of sympathy. The rendering of RSV in verse 33, 'he was deeply moved in spirit', does not give the full force of the Greek, for which Prof. Tasker suggests, 'He was enraged in spirit and troubled Himself' (*TNTC*, p. 140). His anger was roused against the evil powers of death, which caused such distress to mankind, and which He was about to conquer, here by a mighty display of divine power, and finally on the cross by His own death and resurrection.

☐ **STUDY 23   John 11: 45 – 12: 19**

1   Observe the varied effects of the miracle. See especially 11: 45, 46, 47–53, 54; 12: 10, 11, 17–19; and *cf.* Lk. 16: 31. How is it that the same act quickens faith in some, and hatred in others? *Cf.* 11: 47, 48; 12: 11, 19; Mt. 27: 18.

2   12: 1–8. What insights does Mary's action reveal? How far does your love for the Lord lead you to understand Him, and to serve Him without counting the cost?

3 In 11: 47–53 and 12: 12–16 there are two examples of God over-ruling men's words and actions to fulfil His own purposes. What is the real purpose of God to which each points?

Note. 11: 48. The Jewish leaders feared that Jesus might lead a revolt for which the Romans would exact severe punishment.

STUDY 24 John 12: 20–36

The Greeks who inquired for Jesus were a token of the world of people beyond Israel who would be saved through Jesus' atoning death and resurrection (cf. 10: 16; 12: 32). Their coming therefore introduces the consummation of Jesus' work; see verse 23.

1 Give examples of the ways in which you can love your life, or hate it. To whom does Jesus primarily refer in verse 24? In view of this, what is involved in following Him (verse 26)?

2 In what sense did the coming 'hour' (verse 23) bring about the glorifying of the Son of man and of the Father (verse 28)? How did His being lifted up involve the judgment of this world (verses 31–34)?

3 Verses 35, 36 give Jesus' last appeal to the nation. What is meant by walking and believing in the light? Are you doing this?

STUDY 25 John 12: 37–50

This passage presents the problem of unbelief in face of manifest evidence of God's power and presence.

1 Both quotations from Isaiah in verses 38–40 speak of Christ, the latter because Christ's glory is included in the vision of God's glory in Isaiah 6. Who has and who has not 'believed our report'? Why has God blinded their eyes, etc.? Does this apply today to (a) Jews, and (b) non-Jews? Why do you believe?

2 The seriousness of rejecting Jesus is the subject of verses 44–50, in which John summarizes the teaching of Jesus on this matter. Why is it so serious to reject Jesus? See especially verses 45, 46, 50, and compare Pr. 1: 20–33. Why will Jesus' word be the judge (verse 48)?

Notes
1 Verse 42. 'Put out of the synagogue': cf. 9: 22. This was a very severe punishment, involving separation from public worship and from social intercourse.
2 Verse 45. 'Sees': here is the concept of careful observation leading to spiritual insight.

For Studies 26–42 on the second half of John's Gospel see p. 270.

2 KINGS

For Introduction see p. 244.

Analysis

☐ **STUDY 20   2 Kings 1 and 2**

These two chapters contain the last two stories about Elijah.

1   Contrast the end of King Ahaziah with Elijah's end. What was the fundamental difference between these two men? *Cf.* 1 Jn. 2: 15–17; 5: 4.

2   In what three ways was Elisha tested (see 2: 1–15), and what qualities in him does his conduct reveal? Have we the same resolute spirit? See Note 1 below. Elisha's miracles are parables of spiritual truths. What do you learn from this first miracle (2: 19–22)?

Notes

1   2: 9. Elisha wanted to be fully equipped for the high service to which he was called.

2   2: 23–25. 'Small boys': better 'young lads', as in RV mg. These were youths of Bethel, whose attitude reflected the spirit of the place. Coming out to meet Elisha in a large band, they mocked the prophet, who was bald in mourning for his master (*cf.* Jb. 1: 20), and said 'Go up', *i.e.*, 'Ascend to heaven as you say your master did'. It was a grievous insult, and Elisha, righteously angry, invoked the judgment of God upon them. Shaken by the whole episode, he did not enter Bethel but made his way to Carmel.

STUDY 21   2 Kings 3: 1 – 4: 7

1 What was the cause of the attack upon Moab, and how was Elisha brought into the situation? A map should be used to identify the route taken by the attacking armies, and the place where the miracle was wrought. How does the story show what one man of faith can do to save a multitude?

2 How does the story of 4: 1–7 illustrate the working of faith? Was it easy for the woman to do what Elisha bade her do? Has this any lesson for you in your own life?

Notes
1 3: 1. *Cf.* 1: 17. The apparent discrepancy may be explained by the fact that father and son frequently reigned together during the latter part of the father's life.
2 3: 11. 'Who poured water . . .': *i.e.*, he was Elijah's attendant.
3 3: 20. Travellers report that in that region there is water under the sand.

STUDY 22   2 Kings 4: 8–44

1 Verses 8–37. In what ways is the woman of Shunem an example to us? What do you learn about the reasons why God allows His servants to undergo acute suffering? What lessons are to be drawn from Gehazi's failure?

2 What features in Elisha's character are brought out by the incidents in this passage?

Note. Verse 42. The present was for Elisha; and if there was still scarcity of food (verse 38), the gift would be the more precious. But Elisha shared it with all who were with him.

STUDY 23   2 Kings 5: 1 – 6: 7

1 Chapter 5. There are four important figures in this chapter: the captive maid, Naaman, Elisha and Gehazi. What lessons may we learn from each?

2 6: 1–7. Think about this incident in relation to Elisha's position as a spiritual leader. Are there lessons here for the Christian church?

Notes
1 5: 17. The idea in Naaman's mind was that Jehovah, the God of Israel, could not be rightly worshipped except on Israelitish soil. His faith was still very imperfect, as verse 18 also shows.
2 5: 22. 'A talent of silver': *i.e.*, 'four hundred pounds' (Moffatt), a very large sum to be asked for two young men of the sons of the prophets.

STUDY 24   2 Kings 6: 8 – 7: 20

1 6: 8–23. Why was the young man afraid, and why was the prophet not afraid? Have we learned the secret of the conquest of fear? *Cf.* Heb. 11: 27.

2 Observe the severity of the siege, and the greatness of the faith that enabled Elisha to speak as he did in 7: 1. How does the judgment that fell upon the unbelieving officer illustrate the punishment that will follow all wilful unbelief? *Cf.* Mk. 16: 16b; Jn. 3: 36.

3 What lessons do you learn from the part played by the four lepers in this story?

Notes

1 6: 25. 'Ten pounds in silver was paid for the head of an ass and twelve shillings for a pint of doves' dung' (Moffatt).

2 6: 30, 31. Elisha appears to have been sustaining the hopes of the king and people by the promise of divine deliverance. The king's faith now gave way, and he burned with anger against the prophet.

3 7: 1. 'A shekel': 'half-a-crown' (Moffatt).

☐ **STUDY 25 2 Kings 8 and 9**

Today's portion contains (a) two incidents connected with Elisha's ministry; (b) a brief summary of the reigns of two kings of Judah; (c) the story of the revolution under Jehu, through which the house of Ahab was destroyed.

1 8: 1–15. How does the first of these two incidents illustrate God's watchful care over His own? *Cf.* Ps. 33: 18–22; Rom. 8: 28. In the second incident why did Elisha weep? *Cf.* Je. 8: 16 – 9: 1; Lk. 19: 41–44.

2 Ponder the vivid story of the revolution, as given in chapter 9, noticing especially how it began, and the references to the word of God and its fulfilment. *Cf.* Heb. 10: 31; 12: 29; 2 Ki. 10: 30.

3 Consider throughout the history of the kings of Israel and Judah the results of marriage alliances with those who are the enemies of God.

Notes

1 8: 10. The sickness in itself was not fatal, but Elisha was given a vision of other things that would happen, which filled him with horror. Moffatt translates verse 11 thus: 'The man of God's face became rigid with horror, absolute horror.'

2 Verse 13. Hazael was elated at the prospect of doing such deeds.

3 Verse 16. It is important to distinguish between Jehoram, son of Jehoshaphat, king of Judah, and Jehoram (or Joram), son of Ahab, king of Israel. Their reigns were in great measure contemporaneous.

4 Verse 26. Athaliah was the daughter of Ahab and Jezebel, and therefore the granddaughter of Omri. See 1 Ki. 16: 29–31. She married Jehoram, king of Judah (verse 18).

☐ **STUDY 26 2 Kings 10**

1 Trace the course of Jehu's rise to power. Looking back to chapter 9, where was he first anointed, and acclaimed as king? Whither did he then go, striking down in swift succession Jehoram, Ahaziah and

Jezebel? Whom did he further slay, as recorded in 10: 1–14, and by what means?

2 From this account of his reign, what do you learn about Jehu's aim, his character, and his attitude to God?

Note. Verses 9, 10. Jehu quietens the people of Samaria, by reminding them that all that was happening was but the fulfilment of God's word through Elijah. See 1 Ki. 21: 21, 23, 24.

☐ **STUDY 27   2 Kings 11 and 12**

In today's portion we pass from the history of the northern kingdom to the re-establishment in Judah of the worship of Jehovah.

1 What was Athaliah's purpose, and by what two persons, under God, was it brought to nought? What new light does 2 Ch. 22: 11 throw upon the story? Compare with the faith and courage of Jehosheba and Jehoiada that of Moses' parents (*cf.* Heb. 11: 23).

2 What signs of healthy moral and spiritual life do you find in these chapters, and in what respect shortcoming? What part did Joash play in this? See further 2 Ch. 24: 17–24.

☐ **STUDY 28   2 Kings 13 and 14**

This is another composite portion, containing first a brief account of two kings of Israel, Jehoahaz, and Jehoash or Joash (to be distinguished from the king of Judah of the same name); then two incidents connected with Elisha; and finally an account of the reigns of Amaziah, king of Judah, and Jeroboam II of Israel.

1 What evidence is there that in the reign of Jehoahaz Israel was greatly impoverished? Also what reason is assigned for this state of things?

2 In what ways did all four kings, whose reigns are described in chapter 14, fall short of what God required of them?

Notes
1 13: 5. A reference to Jeroboam II; see 14: 27.
2 14: 13. 'Four hundred cubits': about 200 yards.
3 14: 23. Jeroboam II had a long and successful reign, during which the northern kingdom of Israel was greatly extended. See verse 25.
4 14: 25. 'The entrance of Hamath' may refer to the pass between Hermon and Lebanon in the north; 'the sea of Arabah' is the Dead Sea. There is no other reference in Scripture to this particular prophecy of Jonah.

☐ **STUDY 29   2 Kings 15 and 16**

These two chapters cover a period of about eighty years. It is helpful to make a list in parallel columns of the kings of Judah and Israel respectively, mentioned in today's portion, with the length of their reigns.

1   Taking first the kings of Judah, how does Ahaz stand out in sharp contrast to his father Jotham, and his grandfather Azariah (Uzziah)? What two particular acts of folly, one political, the other religious, are recorded of him? *Cf.* Ps. 146: 3–5; Is. 7: 1–9.

2   How long did the dynasty of Jehu continue in Israel? See 10: 30 and Ho. 1: 4. What happened after the dynasty came to an end? What great loss did the northern kingdom suffer in the reign of Pekah? Do you find any good thing recorded of any of the kings of the northern kingdom in these two chapters? *Cf.* Ho. 7: 7; 8: 4; 13: 11.

☐ **STUDY 30   2 Kings 17**

This chapter tells of the end of the northern kingdom of Israel, with the causes of its downfall, and what followed after it.

1   Can you trace a progressive deterioration in Israel's moral and spiritual condition in verses 9–18? Compare the phrase 'did secretly . . .' in verse 9 with 'sold themselves . . .' in verse 17. What are the modern counterparts of the sins which Israel committed? *Cf.* Col. 3: 5; Heb. 12: 25.

2   Consider what great events had taken place in Israel's history in the territory of the northern kingdom, which had brought glory to God, and deliverance to the people. To what condition was it now reduced? *Cf.* 2 Tim. 3: 5; Is. 29: 13.

Notes
1   Verse 2. In what way Hoshea sinned less grievously than preceding kings is not explained.
2   Verses 33, 34. The word 'fear' is used here in two senses; in verse 33 of outward worship, and in verse 34 of heart reverence.

☐ **STUDY 31   2 Kings 18: 1 – 19: 7**

1   What four points about Hezekiah's attitude and conduct with reference to God are mentioned in 18: 3, 5 and 6? Are these things true of us? How did Hezekiah's faith manifest itself in action, and what evidence had he of God's favour and blessing? See verses 4, 7 and 8.

2   In what ways did the Assyrian speaker, Rabshakeh, threaten the people of Israel? What were the reactions to this attack of (a) the people, and (b) Isaiah? *Cf.* Ex. 14: 13; 1 Sa. 17: 44, 45; Dn. 3: 15–18. Are you able to encourage others by your faith, or are you among those that fear and need encouragement?

Notes
1   18: 22. Hezekiah's reforming zeal was no doubt unpopular with many. Rabshakeh knew this, and sought to turn it to advantage for his own ends.
2   19: 3b. A figure of speech denoting a crisis of extreme gravity.

STUDY 32   2 Kings 19: 8–37

1   Comparing Hezekiah's action and words in verses 14–19 with those of the earlier crisis in verses 3, 4, what evidence do you find that Hezekiah's faith had grown stronger?

2   How did Sennacherib appear to merely human judgment? How did he appear as seen by Isaiah with the eyes of faith? Are we learning to look at the world situation today in relation to God? *Cf.* Jn. 14: 1. What does the whole story teach as to the difference which faith in God makes in individual and national life?

Note. Verse 29. The meaning is that only in the third year from the time at which the words were spoken would there be normal sowing and reaping. The fulfilment of the prophet's pronouncement would attest his divinely given authority.

STUDY 33   2 Kings 20 and 21

The events described in chapter 20 happened in the earlier part of Hezekiah's reign before the invasion of Sennacherib (see verses 6 and 13, and also 18: 15, 16), and are introduced here as a kind of appendix to the story of Hezekiah.

1   Put yourself in Hezekiah's place, and try to picture the effect on him of Isaiah's announcement. What did he do (*cf.* Ps. 102: 24), and what did God then do? How would these experiences help to prepare Hezekiah for the greater tests of faith that he was to meet when Sennacherib attacked him? In spite of his faithfulness to God, in what way did Hezekiah fail in the incident recorded in 20: 12–19? *Cf.* Pr. 29: 5. How did Isaiah view the incident, and what word of judgment was given him to speak? For its fulfilment over a century later see chapter 25.

2   Summarize in your own words Manasseh's flagrant idolatry. What judgments did God declare through His prophets? Do you think it can have been easy for the prophets to speak thus? *Cf.* Mi. 3: 8.

Notes

1   20: 12. Merodach-baladan (see Is. 39: 1) was a northern chieftain, who had seized Babylon and was looking round for every possible means of strengthening his position. His reign did not last long, and it would have been folly for Hezekiah to enter into alliance with him.

2   21: 13. The first half of the verse means that Jerusalem will receive the same measure of judgment as Samaria and the house of Ahab. The metaphor in the second half of the verse is a very strong and vivid one.

STUDY 34   2 Kings 22 and 23

1   Make out a list of all that Josiah did, both positively to promote true religion, and negatively to destroy the false. Are our lives marked by a similar eagerness to depart from iniquity and to live

in covenant with God? *Cf.* 2 Cor. 6: 14 – 7: 1. What was the main-spring of Josiah's reforming zeal? *Cf.* Ps. 119: 161b; Is. 66: 2; see also 2 Ki. 23: 25; and contrast the behaviour of Jehoiakim in Je. 36: 23–25.

2 Examine the part played by Huldah the prophetess, and compare with the influence of other women mentioned in previous chapters.

☐ **STUDY 35   2 Kings 24 and 25**

1 Looking back to 23: 31, what four kings reigned between Josiah's death and the fall of Jerusalem? What was the length of their reigns, and what was their record, as described in these chapters?

2 In what ways was Nebuchadnezzar's treatment of Jerusalem after his second capture of it much more severe than when he captured it the first time? What reasons are given in chapter 24 for the captivity? *Cf.* 23: 26, 27; Je. 15: 1–4; Dt. 4: 26, 27. What does this teach us about the end of persistent sinning? Yet what star of hope is seen shining in the closing verses of the book? *Cf.* 2 Sa. 7: 14, 15.

Note. 25: 22. 'Gedaliah the son of Ahikam': see 22: 12; Je. 26: 24. The story of his assassination is told more fully in Je. 40: 1 – 41: 10.

JOHN 13 – 21

☐ **STUDY 26   John 13: 1–20**

1 Verse 13. 'Teacher and Lord.' What degrees of Lordship are revealed in verses 1 and 3? Did Jesus perform the task of a servant in spite of, or because of, His relation to the Father? *Cf.* Phil. 2: 5–8.

2 What important lesson did Jesus teach in response to Peter's interruptions? See verses 8 and 10. *Cf.* Tit. 3: 5; 1 Jn. 1: 7.

3 What further application did Jesus make of His action as an example to His followers? *Cf.* Lk. 22: 22–27. Are you giving sufficient heed to this matter? See verse 17.

Notes
1 Verse 10. 'Bathed': the disciples had been cleansed; all except Judas (verse 11). *Cf.* 15: 3.
2 Verse 20. 'Anyone whom I send': *i.e.*, the apostles and all subsequent witnesses to Christ. So also verse 16.

☐ **STUDY 27   John 13: 21–32**

1 Trace the action of Satan upon the heart of Judas as shown in this Gospel. See 6: 70; 12: 4–6; 13: 2, 27. If the giving of the morsel to him in verse 26 was Jesus' last appeal of love, what state of heart does verse 27a indicate? What connection has verse 30 with 12: 35, 36?

2 Compare verses 31, 32 with 12: 23, 28. Verses 31 and 32a point to the action of the Son and 32b to that of the Father. To what impending events did these words point? How can the Father be glorified in you?

☐ **STUDY 28   John 13: 33 – 14: 14**

1 Trace the connection between 13: 33–37 and 14: 1–6. Where was Jesus going? Why could they not follow until later? To what event does 'I will come again' refer?

2 In what respect were the questions of both Thomas and Philip short-sighted? How is Jesus the way, the truth and the life, especially in relation to the Father?

3 What prospect does Jesus set before His disciples as a consequence of His return to the Father? See verses 12–14. Do you know anything of this in your experience? Why are the works of the believer called 'greater works'?

☐ **STUDY 29   John 14: 15–24**

1 Three times in this passage Jesus speaks of loving Him (verses 15, 21, 23). How does our love for the Lord Jesus show itself? Is this true of you? Since love is personal, can you see to what personal relationship this love leads?

2 In what sense does Jesus 'come' to us (verse 18)? How is this related to the coming of 'another Advocate' (see Note 1)? Give examples of ways in which Jesus proved to be the first 'Advocate'.

3 Why cannot the world 'see' the Spirit or Jesus (verses 17, 19)? *Cf.* 1: 11; 3: 19; 5: 37; 7: 34; 8: 19, 47; 12: 37–40. What explanation did Jesus give here in answer to Judas? How can the eyes of men be opened to see Him?

Notes

1 Verse 16. 'Counsellor': literally, one called to one's side to plead on one's behalf. 'Advocate' is a better translation. *Cf.* 1 Jn. 2: 1.

2 Verse 18. 'Desolate': better, 'bereaved'.

3 Verse 22. *Cf.* 7: 4. The disciples also naturally expected that the Messiah would display His power to the world.

☐ **STUDY 30   John 14: 25 – 15: 8**

1   The disciples were distressed at the thought of Jesus going away and leaving them alone in a hostile world; *cf.* 16: 6. What promises does Jesus give in verses 25–29 to answer their fears? Why does His going to the Father bring greater benefit than if He had remained as He was? What also does verse 31 teach about Christ's reason for facing the cross?

2   What does the parable of the vine teach about (a) the purpose for which the branches exist, (b) the vinedresser's dealing with the branches, and (c) the dependence of the branches upon the vine? With verses 3 and 7 compare 14: 15, 21, 23; see also 8: 31, 32. What kind of fruit do you bear? *Cf.* Gal. 5: 22, 23.

Notes

1 14: 28. 'The Father is greater than I': *cf.* 10: 29, 30. He is not greater in being more *divine*, but in the eternal Father-Son and God-man relationships. (See *NBC*, p. 891.)

2 14: 30. 'The ruler of this world': *cf.* 12: 31; 16: 11; 2 Cor. 4: 4; Eph. 2: 2; 1 Jn. 5: 19. The RSV 'has no power over me' gives the true sense of these words. There is nothing in Jesus over which the devil can claim possession, and therefore domination.

☐ **STUDY 31   John 15: 9–25**

1   People think of the Christian life as a joyless observance of rules. What answer to this idea is contained in these verses? Is it your experience?

2   If we are disciples of Jesus, why must we expect hatred from the world? Why did many hate and persecute Jesus?

3   Love not only feels, but acts. By what actions is (a) the love of the Father shown to the Son, (b) the love of the Son to His disciples, and (c) the love of the disciples to one another? *Cf.* 3: 35; 5: 20; 1 Jn. 3: 16–18.

☐ **STUDY 32   John 15: 26 – 16: 15**

1   What evidence do you find in 16: 1–7 that the disciples were cast down by Jesus' words? Why did He say that He had not spoken of these things before, and why did He speak of them now? Notice,

however, that He did not lighten in any way the dark picture He had drawn, but rather shaded it more deeply (16: 2).

2 What new force, does Jesus say, will be brought to bear upon the world, and through whom (see 15: 26, 27)? What threefold result will follow (16: 8–11)? How would this make Jesus' departure an advantage instead of a loss?

3 What results ought this situation to have upon the disciples (a) in their dependence on the Holy Spirit, and (b) in the place of the Holy Spirit and the Person of Jesus Christ in their thinking? Is this true of us? See 16: 14, 15.

Notes
1 16: 2: 'Put you out of the synagogues': see Note on 12: 42.
2 16: 5. The questions of Thomas (14: 5) and Peter (13: 36, 37) concerned their own following of Jesus. No-one was now asking about the glory to which Christ was going in His return to the Father.
3 16: 8–11. The Holy Spirit will convince men of their false standards of sin, righteousness and judgment (*cf.* Is. 55: 8, 9). He will show them that the essence of sin is unbelief in Christ; that true righteousness is not that of the Pharisees (works of the Law) but the righteousness seen in Christ, and declared in the gospel; and that judgment awaits all who follow the ruler of this world. At Pentecost the heavens were convinced by the Spirit's witness through the apostles, exactly as Jesus says here.
4 16: 13. 'Declare to you the things that are to come': *i.e.*, interpret the significance of Christ's impending crucifixion and resurrection, as well as other divine actions.

☐ **STUDY 33 John 16: 16–33**

1 'A little while'. In the light of verses 16–22 do you consider that this refers to the time between the death of Jesus and His resurrection; between His ascension and Pentecost; or both?

2 Note the RSV in verse 23, 'You will ask me no questions.' With the Spirit to enlighten (*cf.* verses 12–15) and the Father to supply our needs, what do we learn in verses 23–28 about the place of prayer? On what do we rely when we pray in the name of Jesus Christ? *Cf.* 14: 13, 14; 15: 16.

3 In verse 33 Jesus sums up the situation. In what two opposing spheres would the disciples live? What would be their experience in the one and in the other? What can be the ground of your courage and confidence?

☐ **STUDY 34 John 17 (first study)**

Jesus' prayer falls into three divisions: (a) verses 1–5, for Himself; (b) verses 6–19, for the immediate circle of disciples; (c) verses 20–26, for the great company who should afterwards believe.

1   The hour of Jesus' supreme sacrifice has come (verse 1; *cf.* 2: 4; 7: 6, 30; 8: 20; 13: 1). How is this related to the glorifying of the Son and the Father (verses 1–4)? Already the glory of God has been seen in Jesus (1: 18); how is it seen also in His disciples (verse 22)? When will they see the full glory of the Son (verses 5, 24)?

2   In verses 6–14 note how many things Jesus has already done for His disciples.

3   What does our Lord pray that the Father will do for those whom He has given Him? Is this prayer being answered in you? Are you 'consecrated in truth' (verse 19)?

Notes
1   Verse 2. 'Power': better, 'authority', as in RV. The whole of humanity lies within the sphere of Christ's commission. *Cf.* Ps. 2: 8; Mt. 28: 18, 19.
2   Verse 5. A prayer that the glory of which for a time He had 'emptied himself'(Phil. 2: 6, 7) might be restored to Him.
3   Verses 17, 19. Note the repetition of the word 'to consecrate'. Jesus consecrated Himself to the holy Father in fulfilment of His perfect will, particularly in offering Himself as the sacrifice for sin. *Cf.* Heb. 10: 5–10. This shows what true consecration involves.

☐   **STUDY 35   John 17 (second study)**

1   What is our relationship to the world? How should we ourselves pray regarding people in the world?

2   Verses 20–23. Is the Lord praying for the uniting of all branches of the Christian church as in the ecumenical movement? What is the object of His prayer? What will its fuller realization mean?

3   Observe the significance of the 'word' or 'words' of the Father and the Son in this passage.

☐   **STUDY 36   John 18: 1–27**

Jesus' arrest and trial before Caiaphas.

1   In verses 4–11 and 19–23 what qualities of our Lord's character appear in relation to (a) those who came to arrest Him, (b) His disciples, and (c) His accusers?

2   How did Peter's own actions contribute to his fall? Of what was he afraid? Does fear ever prevent you from declaring your association with Jesus Christ?

Note. Verses 5, 6, 8. 'I am he': the thrice-repeated use of this phrase points to its special significance. It is virtually a reiteration of the divine name, 'I AM'. *Cf.* Ex. 3: 14; Jn. 8: 58. Note the effect of Christ's statement on the hearers.

☐ **STUDY 37   John 18: 28 – 19: 16**

The trial before Pilate.

1   Trace through this passage the attempts made by Pilate to spare
Jesus from death, and the steps taken by the Jews to counter his
efforts. The full charge brought against Jesus is given in Lk. 23: 2.
(Note the Jews' use of both religious and political threats to overcome Pilate's resistance; see 19: 7, 12.) What features of the character of Pilate and of the Jews are revealed here? Could we be guilty
of similar injustice?

2   'The King of the Jews.' Note how this title forms the central
interest from 18: 33 to 19: 22. What is the real nature of Jesus'
Kingship? How does it differ from the world's? How is Jesus' royal
dignity shown here? How does the use of the title reveal the sin of
the Jews, and the glory of Jesus' sacrifice?

Notes
1   18: 28. 'Praetorium': the headquarters of the Roman governor.
2   18: 31b. The Romans did not allow the Jews to inflict capital punishment.
Hence Pilate's words in 19: 6 imply that there was no ground in Roman
law for Jesus' death. However he spoke a deeper truth than he realized.

☐ **STUDY 38   John 19: 17–37**

1   The story of the crucifixion is told in seven incidents, namely
verses 17–18, 19–22, 23–24, 25–27, 28–29, 30, 31–37. How does each
incident manifest some fresh aspect of the glory of the suffering
Saviour?

2   Which scriptures are quoted in this portion as having found
fulfilment in this hour? To which aspects of Jesus' sufferings and of
His saving work do they point?

☐ **STUDY 39   John 19: 38 – 20: 10**

1   What made both Joseph of Arimathea and Nicodemus now
come out into the open? With 19: 38 *cf.* Lk. 23: 50, 51; and trace
Nicodemus' growing faith, 3: 1–15; 7: 45–52. Both were members
of the Sanhedrin, the Council of the Jews which had condemned
Jesus.

2   20: 1–10. How do these verses show that the disciples were not
expecting the resurrection of the Lord? What does the description
of Peter and John's visit to the tomb reveal about each of their
respective temperaments? What was it that John believed?

Notes
1   19: 39. 'About a hundred pounds' weight': an exceptionally lavish
amount.

2 20: 5, 7. The position of the clothes showed that they had not been unwound from Jesus' body. He had gone out, just as later He came in, where the doors were shut, without the doors being opened (20: 19, 26).

☐ **STUDY 40 John 20: 11–31**

1 Why was Mary so concerned that the body had gone from the tomb? What did Jesus convey to her when He said 'Mary'? Why did He say, 'Do not hold me'? Is it possible for us to miss the best in the Lord while holding on to the good?

2 Does verse 29 show that the disciples were still doubting? What convinced them that Jesus was truly raised from the dead? Why was Thomas moved to make the complete avowal of faith, to which none of the others had yet attained? Was it only that he saw Jesus? How can one who has not seen Him be led to faith in the risen Lord (verses 29–31)?

3 In verses 21–23 the risen Christ commissions His apostles. By what authority, with what power, and for what purpose does He send them?

Note. Verse 17. Note the distinction, 'my Father and your Father'. Jesus never said of Himself and His disciples, 'Our Father', as though their relation to God was the same as His. He is the only begotten Son; we are sons of God 'in Him'.

☐ **STUDY 41 John 21: 1–14**

1 Compare this passage with Lk. 5: 1–11, noting the similarities and the differences. Why did the disciples take up their old work again? What did they learn from this experience?

2 What did the Lord reveal here (a) about Himself, (b) about the work which the disciples were to do? How does this revelation of the risen Lord affect your own life and work?

Note. Verse 14. 'The third time': first time, 20: 19–23; second time, 20: 24–29; third time, now in Galilee. See Mk. 16: 7. Probably the third recorded by this Gospel is meant here.

☐ **STUDY 42 John 21: 15–25**

1 What is the significance of (a) Jesus' use of the name Simon in addressing Peter (*cf.* 1: 42); (b) the phrase 'more than these' (verse 15; *cf.* Mk. 10: 28–30; 14: 29); (c) Jesus asking Peter three times, 'Do you love me?' (*cf.* 13: 38)?

2 Though Peter had failed, Jesus re-commissioned him. What does this teach about (a) the Lord's nature, (b) Peter's spiritual condition?

Can you expect always to be restored after a fall? What does the Lord require from you?

3 What may we learn from verses 18–23 about (a) the different ways in which the Lord directs the life of each one of His people; (b) what our own main concern is to be?

Notes
1 Verses 18, 19. According to tradition Peter died as a martyr in Rome.
2 Verse 23. A statement introduced to correct a current misunderstanding of what the Lord had said about John.

ISAIAH 1 - 39

Introduction

Isaiah, the 'evangelical prophet', began his ministry at the end of Uzziah's reign, and continued through the reigns of Jotham, Ahaz and Hezekiah. A Jewish tradition, to which allusion is perhaps made in Heb. 11: 37, states that he was slain in the reign of Manasseh by being sawn asunder. He was a man of outstanding faith in God, and came to exercise a large influence upon his fellow-countrymen. He had to contend with many difficulties, for the moral and spiritual condition of the people was corrupt. The rich oppressed the poor, and revelled in wanton luxury; justice was shamelessly bought and sold. When in distress, men turned to idols; and when in danger, they sought alliances with heathen powers. Isaiah urged a quiet trust in Jehovah, as the only sure path of safety; and when, in the supreme crisis of the Assyrian invasion, his counsel was followed, it was triumphantly vindicated in the destruction of the Assyrian army.

Isaiah spoke much of impending judgment; but he foresaw also the coming of the Messiah, and the establishment of His kingdom. His interest was not confined to his own nation of Judah only. He prophesied also concerning the northern kingdom of Israel (whose overthrow he witnessed), and the heathen nations surrounding Palestine.

The last twenty-seven chapters (40–66) contain a very remarkable group of prophecies, spoken primarily for the comfort and warning of those who lived in the period of the Jewish captivity in Babylon after the destruction of Jerusalem by Nebuchadnezzar about 150 years after Isaiah's time. It is not possible here to discuss the modern contention that chapters 40–66 are not the work of Isaiah, but of one or more prophets who lived in the period of exile, or later. The problem is dealt with quite fully in the Introduction to Isaiah in *The New Bible Commentary*, where the arguments adduced in favour of and against the unity of the book are carefully set down and analysed. Suffice it to say here that these studies are based upon the view, not lightly held, and supported by ancient Jewish tradition, and by the writers of the New Testament, that Isaiah was the author of the whole book. He had already foreseen in the vision of 13: 1 – 14: 23 (to which his name is attached; see 13: 1) and in other visions (*e.g.*, 21: 1–10; 35; 39: 6) the rise of Babylon to power and glory, and then her downfall, and the release of her Jewish captives. But in these later prophecies the glad message of redemption is revealed to him in far greater fullness. He takes his stand in prophetic vision in that later age, and declares the messages which God puts into his heart and upon his lips.

The chapters fall into three main sections (see Analysis), each ending with a statement of the doom of the wicked (48: 22; 57: 20, 21; 66: 24). Embedded in these chapters are four prophecies, usually known as the 'Servant' passages (see Analysis), in which the prophet describes God's ideal Servant, and, in so doing, draws a perfect picture of the Lord Jesus Christ. This is an illustration of a notable feature of the prophecies of these chapters, that they look far beyond the period of the return under Cyrus to the coming of Jesus Christ, and the final events of this present age. While spoken primarily to and of Israel, they have a message to all who belong to Christ. The triumphant faith in God, the revelation of God's character, and of the principles of His working, the insight into the human heart in its sin and weakness, the 'exceeding great and precious promises', with which these chapters abound, these and other features make this part of Scripture a veritable mine of wealth to the Christian reader.

Analysis

1	Introductory. God's controversy with His people.
2 – 4	Prophecies of judgment, lying between two Messianic oracles.
5	The Song of the Vineyard. A series of woes. Vision of an invading army.
6	Isaiah's call.

7: 1 – 10: 4	Events connected with the alliance of Ephraim (*i.e.*, northern Israel) and Syria against Judah, and prophecies arising out of them, some Messianic.
10: 5–34	Assyrian invasion of Judah, and its results (a) for Assyria, (b) for Judah.
11 – 12	Messianic prophecies.
13 – 23	Prophecies against the nations, except 22: 1–14 (Jerusalem) and 22: 15–25 (Shebna and Eliakim).
24 – 27	Prophecies of the Day of the Lord, in its twofold aspect of world judgment, and deliverance for Israel.
28 – 33	Prophecies connected with a proposed alliance with Egypt. Some speak of judgment, others of deliverance, and of Messiah's coming.
34 – 35	Vengeance upon Edom, contrasted with the salvation of the redeemed of the Lord, as they return from exile.
36 – 39	Historical.
40 – 48	The glad tidings of Israel's redemption from captivity through the agency of Cyrus. The supremacy of Jehovah over the nations and their gods.
	42: 1–7 The first of the 'Servant' passages.
49 – 57	Messages of encouragement and comfort, with rebuke of those who practise evil.
	49: 1–9 ⎫ The second, third and fourth of 50: 4–9 ⎬ the 'Servant' passages. 52: 13 – 53; 12 ⎭
58 – 66	Rebuke of sin. Visions of Zion's glory. Prayer for God's intervention, and God's answer, that the people will be sifted. The true Israel will inherit 'the new heavens and the new earth', and those who refuse to turn to God will be destroyed.

☐ **STUDY 1 Isaiah 1**

1 What were the sins that had brought God's judgment on the nation of Israel? See verses 2, 4, 13b, 15. Why should God condemn their formal religious observances (verses 10–17)? See also Ps. 40: 6–9; Am. 5: 21–24; Mi. 6: 6–8.

2 What is the double purpose of God's judgment revealed in verses 24–31? Can you link it with verses 19 and 20?

Notes

1 Verses 5, 6. Sinful Israel is pictured as a body suffering all over from sword wounds, scourge bruises, and abscesses.

2 Verse 10. In God's sight His people are as depraved as Sodom and Gomorrah. *Cf.* 3: 9; Mt. 11: 23, 24.

3 Verse 22. Silver and wine are probably metaphors for the leaders of the nation.

☐ **STUDY 2 Isaiah 2 – 4**

The prophet's lofty vision of future possibility in 2: 2–5 gives way to a picture of coming judgment in 2: 6–22, made inevitable by man's failure. From a description of the anarchy (3: 1–8) which will result from the prevalent sins of the ruling class, both men and women (3: 9 – 4: 1), he turns to a more confident expectation of the glory which will follow the judgment (4: 2–6).

1 Try to build a comprehensive picture of the hope for the future given in 2: 2–5 and 4: 2–6. What is said about the word of the Lord, the peace of the world, the holiness of God's people, and their blessedness under His protecting care?

2 Can you detect from these chapters what Isaiah regarded as the greatest sin, and why it is so abominable?

Notes
1 2: 2–4. A prophecy almost identical with Mi. 4: 1–3, and probably borrowed by Micah from Isaiah.
2 2: 6. The striking of hands may refer not only to friendship but to trade bargaining. Commercial greed is further condemned in verse 7a.
3 3: 12. A reference to the childishness and effeminacy of King Ahaz.

☐ **STUDY 3 Isaiah 5**

1 Compare Isaiah's song of the vineyard with Christ's parables of the wicked husbandmen (Mk. 12: 1–9) and the barren fig tree (Lk. 13: 6–9). Note the differences, and then work out the one great lesson taught in all three passages. How can it be applied to our lives today? *Cf.* Jn. 15: 8.

2 Make a list of the six 'Woes' in verses 8–24, finding twentieth-century words to describe each sin denounced.

Note. Verse 14. 'Sheol' (Greek 'Hades') is the place where all the dead go. It is depicted as a dim and shadowy underworld.

☐ **STUDY 4 Isaiah 6**

1 What did Isaiah's vision of God in His glory teach him (a) about the character of God, and (b) about himself and his needs? What may this teach us concerning God's provision of cleansing for sinners who deserve judgment?

2 How was Isaiah prepared for his task of carrying God's message to his own people? Consider the message itself; what does it reveal of the inevitable outcome of rebellion against God? *Cf.* Acts 28: 23–28.

Note. Verses 9, 10. In seeking to understand these verses (with which *cf.* Mk. 4: 10–12, where Jesus quotes them), remember these two facts:
(a) Although the Word is preached in order to bring salvation to those who will hear, it inevitably brings condemnation to those who will not. *Cf.* Jn. 3: 16–21.

(b) The Old Testament, with its unshakable faith in God's sovereignty, often refuses to distinguish between intention and inevitable result, between God's permissive and directive will. Thus, to say 'Preach to them and they will not respond' could equally well be expressed, 'Preach to them in order that they may not respond.'

☐ **STUDY 5 Isaiah 7: 1 – 8: 15**

Isaiah now turns his attention from the internal condition of Judah to the realm of international politics. The historical background of chapters 7: 1 – 10: 4 is the so-called Syro-Ephraimitic confederacy, when King Rezin of Syria and King Pekah of Israel conspired against Judah (735 BC). Ahaz of Judah, overcome with panic (7: 2), rejected the counsel of Isaiah that he should trust in God (7: 3, 4), and appealed to King Tiglath-Pileser of Assyria, an act which Isaiah predicted would have disastrous consequences in the end, even though at first apparently successful (7: 17 – 8: 4).

1 What did Ahaz lose, both personally and politically, through his refusal to trust in the Lord?

2 How is the historical 'sign' to be given to Ahaz a foreshadowing of the future coming of the Messiah? Cf. Mt. 1: 21–23. In daily experience do you know Christ as 'Immanuel'—'God with us'?

3 How could the Lord be both a sanctuary and a stumbling-block (8: 13–15), and how may He be to us the former and not the latter? Cf. 1 Pet. 2: 7, 8.

Notes
1 The two names, Shear-jashub ('A remnant shall return') and Maher-shalal-hash-baz ('Speed, spoil, haste, prey'), sum up Isaiah's double message of doom and hope.
2 7: 3. Ahaz was probably making preparation for the siege when Isaiah met him.
3 7: 14–16. The primary meaning seems to be that before a certain child (as yet unborn) emerges from infancy, his diet will have to be limited to curds and honey, since the devastated land will yield no better food (7: 21, 22). But the child's remarkable name, and the mention of the 'young woman' or 'virgin' (mg.; cf. Mt. 1) who is to be his mother, provide a prophetic reference to the Messiah.
4 8: 6. 'The waters of Shiloah': i.e., the water supplies of Jerusalem, dependent on subterranean springs and reservoirs under the Temple area, here used symbolically of God's providence. The phrase 'this people' must refer either to Israel or a pro-Syrian party in Judah, unless, as some think, the verb Isaiah used was not the word 'rejoice' (AV, RV), but a word of similar letters meaning 'faint before' ('melt in fear before', RSV).

☐ **STUDY 6 Isaiah 8: 16 – 10: 4**

The prophet will withdraw his disciples, and the elect remnant will thus take shape (8: 16–18). The dark days (8: 19–22) will end in the coming of a great light, the advent of the Messiah (9: 1–7). The remainder of chapter 9 is a prophecy of judgment upon the northern kingdom of Israel. Let Judah then beware (10: 1–4)!

1   When disaster comes, and God seems to have hidden His face, what is man tempted to do (8: 19)? *Cf.* Lv. 19: 31; 1 Sa. 28: 6, 7. What must the child of God do in such a case? What test does Isaiah propose for spiritist teachings?

2   Contrast the condition of things under God's anger (8: 21, 22; 9: 8 – 10: 4) with Isaiah's picture of Messiah's reign (9: 1–7). What do the names given to the coming King in 9: 6 reveal of His nature?

Note. 9: 1. The anguish of the northern kingdom 'in the former time' no doubt refers to Tiglath-Pileser's invasion mentioned in 2 Ki. 15: 29. 'The latter time', though future to the prophet, is described with the past tense of prophetic certainty. For the fulfilment, in part, of the prophecy, see Mt. 4: 15, 16.

☐ **STUDY 7   Isaiah 10: 5–34**

A prophecy of the Assyrian invasion of Judah.

1   Contrast the invasion as seen in the mind of the Assyrian king (verses 7–10, 13, 14), and as seen in the purpose of God (verses 5, 6, 12, 16–19). How does this passage help us to understand how the holy God can use evil men or nations to carry out His purposes?

2   In the stress of the trial it might have seemed that God had cast off His people. But was it so (verses 20–23)? *Cf.* Rom. 9: 27–29. What was the purpose of God's chastening?

3   How does today's portion make more clear the two predictions implied in the names of the prophet's two sons? See Study 5, Note 1.

Notes
1   Verse 17. 'The light of Israel' and 'his Holy One' are names for God.
2   Verse 20. 'Him that smote them': *i.e.*, the king of Assyria. The 'remnant' will have learned the lesson Ahaz had failed to learn.
3   Verses 28–32. A vivid picture of the approach of the enemy, checked only at the very walls of Jerusalem.

☐ **STUDY 8   Isaiah 11 and 12**

The Assyrian cedar would be irrevocably felled, but out of the stump of the pollarded Judaean tree will come forth a shoot—the Messiah, in whom Isaiah's hope for the future is centred. His glorious reign (11) is considered (a) in relation to human society (2–5); (b) in relation to the brute creation (6–9); and (c) in relation to world history (10–16). There follows (12: 1–6) a song of thanksgiving to God for His forgiveness, together with a vision of a united Israel (*cf.* 11: 13) enjoying the blessings of salvation, and engaging in missionary activity among the nations.

1   What are to be the characteristics of the coming Messiah (11: 1–5)? Compare this picture of His reign with 9: 1–7, and notice any new truths brought out.

2   Chapter 12 is the song of those who have discovered that God's anger is turned away from them. What results of salvation are mentioned here, and are you experiencing them all?

☐ **STUDY 9   Isaiah 13: 1 – 14: 23**

Here we have the Book of Immanuel, and enter what has been called the 'jungle of prophecy' (chapters 13–25). See Analysis. It contains the 'burdens of the Lord', oracles concerning foreign nations, many parts of which are now obscure. The first oracle concerns Babylon, and is directed first against the city (13: 1 – 14: 2), and second, against the king (14: 3–23). Its predictions have been literally fulfilled.

1   For what sins was Babylon condemned by God (14: 5, 6, 12–14)? How did God administer judgment?

2   In what respects may Babylon be regarded as a picture of the world in opposition to God (as Jerusalem or Zion is a picture of God's people), and the king of Babylon a picture of Satan, the prince of this world? Cf. Gn. 11: 1–9; 2 Thes. 2: 4; Rev. 18: 2, 3.

Notes
1   13: 2–6. 'The day of the Lord' is the day of His manifestation and here denotes the day of His vengeance upon Babylon.
2   13: 12. The population will be so reduced, that men will be scarcer than gold.
3   14: 9–17. The departed spirits in Sheol assemble, surprised and scornful, to greet the arrival of the king whose pomp is now stripped from him.

☐ **STUDY 10   Isaiah 14: 24 – 16: 14**

A series of denunciatory oracles directed against Assyria (14: 24–27), Philistia (14: 28–32), and Moab (15; 16).

1   14: 24–27. What two attributes of God are emphasized in these verses? How do they encourage us to trust in His Word?

2   In the prophecy against Moab consider (a) the severity of the judgment, (b) the sympathy of the prophet with Moab in her sufferings, and (c) the reason why her doom is inevitable. Are you moved by the thought of the judgment which awaits those who reject Christ?

Notes
1   14: 29. 'The rod which smote you is broken': a reference probably to the death of Tiglath-Pileser of Assyria who died just before Ahaz. However, it was no use rejoicing at this, for the power of Assyria would be revived in a form more deadly than ever.
2   14: 30–32. The meaning is that while even the poorest in Judah shall be secure (verses 30a and 32), Philistia shall be destroyed.
3   15. The proper names are Moabite towns, known and unknown. On the signs of grief and mourning in verses 2 and 3, cf. 22: 12; Mi. 1: 16.
4   16: 1–5. The Moabites are advised to send tribute in the form of lambs (cf. 2 Ki. 3: 4) to the king of Judah. Verses 3–5 is the Moabites' plea for refuge.

☐ **STUDY 11   Isaiah 17–19**

Oracles concerning Damascus (*i.e.*, Syria) and Ephraim, Ethiopia, and Egypt, with a short oracle (17: 12–14) prophesying the overthrow of the Assyrian hosts.

1   How is Ephraim's sin described in 17: 10, together with its inevitable issue? *Cf.* Dt. 8: 19, 20.

2   Gather out from these chapters what is said of the results of God's judgment in causing men to turn to Him. What encouragements for missionary work, especially in certain countries, may be derived from these chapters?

3   Contrast in chapter 18 man's scheming and planning with God's attitude of quiet watchfulness, knowing what He will do (verses 4–6). *Cf.* Ps. 2: 1–5.

Note. 18: 1, 2. A description of Ethiopia, whose ambassadors have come to consult with Judah about plans to resist Assyria. The 'whirring wings' is probably an allusion to the swarms of insects which infest the land. Isaiah gives the ambassadors a message to take back (verses 2b–7), that God is watching, and will shortly deal with the Assyrian menace.

☐ **STUDY 12   Isaiah 20: 1 – 22: 14**

The story of an acted prophecy on the futility of reliance upon Egypt (20) is followed by four oracles concerning Babylon (21: 1–10), Edom (21: 11, 12), Arabia (21: 13–17), and Jerusalem (22: 1–14).

1   In what ways did Isaiah's responsibility to convey God's message prove demanding and costly? Are you prepared to sacrifice your pride in your service for God (chapter 20)? Do you spare time to wait on God (21: 8, 12)?

2   In what two respects does Isaiah in 22: 1–14 find fault with the people of Jerusalem? Do you find the same spirit prevalent today?

3   In what ways does this passage teach us that God is behind the events of history, knowing all beforehand, and carrying out His purposes?

Note. 22: 1–3. The prophet bewails the conduct of the people, thronging the house-tops, shouting and rejoicing when calamity was near. 'Without the bow' (which had been cast aside) they were captured.

☐ **STUDY 13   Isaiah 22: 15 – 23: 18**

1   Why did God depose Shebna and put Eliakim in his place? If God can say of you 'my servant', how are you filling your position? *Cf.* Mt. 24: 45–51.

2 Isaiah foresees a day when Tyre's riches will be no longer hoarded for her own selfish enjoyment, but will be lavished upon Jehovah and His people. If then he is not condemning wealth in itself as evil, what is he attacking in the earlier part of the chapter? What should be the Christian's attitude towards wealth and material prosperity? *Cf.* 1 Tim. 6: 6-10, 17-19.

STUDY 14 Isaiah 24 and 25

Chapter 24 begins the long apocalyptic vision of the Day of the Lord which continues until chapter 27. It seems impossible to give it any certain historical background, and it was probably intended to be an ideal description of the last great judgment which will engulf the whole world. The horizon is very black except for the bright gleam of light which appears in verse 23, and which leads on to the burst of praise in chapter 25, just as chapter 12 follows chapter 11. First in his own name (25), and then in the name of the redeemed community (26), the prophet gives thanks for their certain deliverance from the final judgment and for their everlasting bliss and security.

1 In chapter 24 contrast the emotions of unbelievers when faced with the calamity of God's judgment with the reactions of believers. Can you still praise God in the midst of seeming disaster? *Cf.* Hab. 3: 16-19.

2 What does chapter 25 teach us about God's 'faithful and sure' plans for this world and for His people?

3 Compare this Old Testament picture of God's ultimate purpose for His people with the New Testament one in Rev. 7: 15-17; 21: 1-4.

Note. 25: 2. In this verse, as in 24: 10, 12 and 26: 5, 6, 'the city' refers to no special town, but to any stronghold of opposition to God, in contrast to God's 'strong city' (26: 1). The former will be 'made a heap', but the latter fortified with impregnable bulwarks.

STUDY 15 Isaiah 26 and 27

1 Think over the attitudes of heart described in 26: 3, 4, 8, 9, 13 and 19, and ask yourself if you share this trust and faith in God. What should be the response of God's people to His mercy and judgment?

2 How does chapter 27 express the principle underlying God's chastisement of His people, and also His ultimate purpose?

Notes
1 26: 19. The prophet's answer to the people's plaint is the promise of resurrection. His words here and in 25: 8 are among the clearest utterances of the Old Testament upon that subject.
2 27: 1. The three monsters represent three world powers, probably Assyria, Babylon and Egypt.

☐ **STUDY 16   Isaiah 28**

This is the first of four chapters of warning to Judah. Their main theme is the folly of seeking help from Egypt. Warnings of terrible judgment (observe the recurrence of the word 'woe', see 28: 1; 29: 1, 15; 30: 1; 31: 1) intermingle with assurances of God's intervention in mercy. The divisions of chapter 28 are as follows: verses 1–4, judgment upon Samaria; verses 5, 6, after the judgment; verses 7–13, the drunken rulers of Judah rebuked; verses 14–23, the coming storm of God's judgment will sweep away all man-made policies; verses 23–29, if the farmer acts with wisdom, how much more God?

1   How many consequences of intemperance can you discern in verses 1–4, 7 and 8? What was God's message to His intemperate people, and why would they not listen (verses 9–15)?

2   What do verses 16–29 teach us about the inevitable triumph of God's will in human affairs, and the futility of unbelief and rebellion? How does the parable in verses 23–29 encourage us to see that God has foreseen and arranged all?   •

3   What foreshadowing of Christ is there in the final fulfilment of God's plans? *Cf.* verse 16; 1 Pet. 2: 6, 7; Acts 4: 11; Mt. 21: 42.

Note. Verses 15, 18. Isaiah calls the proposed alliance with Egypt 'a covenant with death'. 'The overflowing scourge' is Assyria.

☐ **STUDY 17   Isaiah 29: 1 – 30: 17**

1   29: 9–16. What were the reasons for the people's spiritual blindness and lack of spiritual discernment, and in what ways did they show this? What causes the spiritual transformation of verses 17–22? See verses 18, 24.

2   On what various grounds does Isaiah urge upon his hearers that they should rely upon God rather than upon Egypt? Trace out in 30: 8–17 the respective issues of the two ways.

3   Observe the contrast between the extreme distress of Jerusalem in 29: 2–4, and her complete triumph in 29: 5–8. How may this encourage us in times of severe trial?

Note. 29: 1–8. 'Ariel' is a name for Jerusalem. It may mean 'lion of God' or, as is more probable here, 'hearth of God' (RV mg.). Jerusalem will become an altar hearth soaked with the blood of many victims.

☐ **STUDY 18   Isaiah 30: 18 – 32: 20**

1   What blessings does God promise to His people after their trials? *Cf.* 30: 18–29; 32: 1–8, 15–20. How has the promise of a Teacher been fulfilled to us in Christ? Look up Jn. 14: 26; 16: 13, in this connection. Are we sensitive to the promptings of the Holy Spirit (30: 21)?

2 Many trusted in Egypt because she seemed strong (31: 1). How does Isaiah here show the folly of this, as compared with trusting the Lord?

Notes

1 30: 25, 26. A poetic description of the blessings of the new age, to be interpreted symbolically as showing the abundance of God's provision. For the phrase 'when the towers fall', *cf.* 2: 11–17.

2 30: 27–33. Notice the wealth of imaginative metaphor—the storm, the flood, the bridle. The meaning of verse 32 is not fully clear. Moffatt renders 'He clubs them down to peals of merry music'. 'Topheth' (verse 33, mg.) was the name given to the valley of Hinnom outside Jerusalem, where the foul rites of human sacrifice were practised in honour of the god Molech. Its original meaning seems to have been 'fire place', and Isaiah declares that God has prepared such a place for a great holocaust in honour of the king (of Assyria). There is a play upon words in the Hebrew, for the word for 'king' is *melek* (= Molech).

☐ STUDY 19 Isaiah 33–35

The opening verses of chapter 33 reflect the excitement and panic which preceded Sennacherib's approach (verses 7–9) and the prophet's triumphant faith that the proud Assyrian would suffer defeat (verses 1–6, 10–12). The remainder of the chapter shows the profound effects of this deliverance, and paints a glowing picture of the coming kingdom. Chapters 34 and 35 present a striking contrast between the fearful doom of God's enemies, symbolized by Edom (34), and the glorious future which awaits God's redeemed people (35).

1 In the picture of the Messiah's kingdom, given in 33: 14–24, (a) what are the characteristics of His people, (b) what will the Lord be to them, and (c) what blessings will they enjoy?

2 Applied spiritually, what blessings are spoken of in chapter 35 which are available to believers now? In particular, can you discover in verses 8–10 four or five characteristics of the 'highway', *i.e.*, the Christian life?

Notes

1 33: 18, 19. The things that terrified them before, such as Assyrian officials counting the tribute, will all belong to the past.

2 34: 6, 7. God's judgment of Edom pictured as a sacrifice in Bozrah, an Edomite city.

3 34: 16. 'The book of the Lord': this probably refers to a collection of Isaiah's previous prophecies. None of them shall fail. The Spirit of God will accomplish in history what the mouth of God's servant has declared in prophecy. *Cf.* 55: 11; Je. 1: 9, 10.

☐ STUDY 20 Isaiah 36 and 37

We have now reached 701 BC, the year of Sennacherib's siege of Jerusalem, so long predicted. Chapters 36–39 repeat, with a few omissions and additions, the history recorded in 2 Ki. 18: 13 – 20: 11. The course of events seems to have been as follows: (1) After receiving the tribute demanded (2 Ki. 18: 14–16),

Sennacherib sent three envoys with an army to demand further the surrender of Jerusalem (36: 1 – 37: 7). (2) This was refused and the Assyrian troops withdrew, but Sennacherib sent a letter to Hezekiah renewing his demands (37: 8–35). This also was rejected, and the chapter concludes with a brief account of how God fulfilled His word (37: 36–38).

1 36: 4–10, 13–20. How did the Rabshakeh try to shake the confidence of the defenders of Jerusalem in the power of God to save them? What fact did he ignore which invalidated the basic assumption of his argument? Cf. 37: 18–20, 23–29.

2 Both Hezekiah and Isaiah recognized in Sennacherib's challenge a blasphemous insult to the living God (37: 6, 7, 17, 23). How did this give them confidence? Cf. 1 Sa. 17: 26, 36, 45–47.

Notes

1 36: 1. The chronological note is wrong, for 701 BC was Hezekiah's twenty-sixth year. Possibly the note belongs properly to 38: 1, and has become misplaced. See Note under Study 21 below.

2 36: 2, 3. Rabshakeh was the title of the Assyrian chief-captain, second to the Tartan or commander-in-chief. As there were three envoys (2 Ki. 18: 17), so three Jewish high officials were sent to meet them.

3 36: 7. Whether in ignorance or in subtlety, the Rabshakeh spoke of Hezekiah's religious reformation (2 Ki. 18: 4), as if it had been an act of disrespect towards God. Possibly to a heathen mind it appeared in that light.

☐ **STUDY 21 Isaiah 38 and 39**

The events of these chapters preceded Sennacherib's invasion. Hezekiah reigned twenty-nine years (2 Ki. 18: 2). He probably fell ill in the fourteenth year of his reign. See Note on 36: 1 in Study 20 above.

1 How does chapter 38 show forth (a) the power of prayer (cf. Jas. 5: 16b), (b) a loving purpose behind suffering (cf. Ps. 119: 71, 75), (c) the completeness of God's forgiveness (cf. Ps. 103: 12; Mi. 7: 19), (d) the duty of praise (cf. Ps. 13: 6)?

2 Wherein lay Hezekiah's sin in displaying his royal treasures and military might to the envoys of Merodach-baladan? Cf. 2 Ch. 32: 25, 31. How does the incident reveal what was in his heart?

Notes

1 38: 7, 8. The sign was a miraculous alteration of the shadow on the sun-dial, and not necessarily of the sun in the sky. It may have been caused by eclipse or reflection, and appears to have been a local phenomenon only (cf. 2 Ch. 32: 31).

2 38: 11 and 18. The thought that death cut them off from God made it a cause of dread to Old Testament believers. Contrast 1 Cor. 15: 20, 55, 56.

3 39: 1. Merodach-baladan made himself king of Babylon in defiance of Assyria in 721 BC, but was taken captive by the Assyrian king Sargon in 709. Before his downfall he sought to secure himself against Assyria by foreign alliances, one of which was with Judah in 714. Hezekiah's sickness and remarkable recovery gave him occasion to make a first approach. Cf. 2 Ch. 32: 31.

For Studies 22–42 on Isaiah see p. 294.

THE EPISTLES OF JOHN

Introduction

1 John and the Epistle to the Hebrews are the only two New Testament letters written anonymously; and in 2 and 3 John, the author merely introduces himself as 'the elder'. It is clear, however, that the three Johannine Epistles are by the same person, and there is a very strong case for saying that it is the same person as the author of John's Gospel. The evidence of the letters themselves, and the witness of early Christians, suggest that the writer is the apostle John. He writes as an eye-witness who has personally known the Lord (1: 1–4; 4: 14). He writes as a teacher with great, indeed, with apostolic authority (2: 8, 17; 3: 6; 4: 1; 5: 20, 21). He writes as a pastor, with a deep concern both to defend and confirm the faith of the church (2: 1, 26; 4: 1–6; 2 Jn. 9; 3 Jn. 4).

In the first Epistle, John sets forth three marks of a true knowledge of God and of fellowship with God. These marks are, first, righteousness of life, second, brotherly love, and third, faith in Jesus as God incarnate. Such characteristics distinguish true Christians from false teachers who, for all their lofty profession and Christian language, neither believe nor obey the truth.

In 2 and 3 John, the writer deals with the problem of giving hospitality to visiting Christians. False teachers were abusing the generosity of Christian people, and some advice was needed to help Christians in dealing with the situation.

Analysis of 1 John

2:7–11   (ii) Brotherly love.

2:12–14   Digression on the church.

2:15–17   Digression on the world.

2:18–27   (iii) Confession that Jesus Christ is come in the flesh.

2:28 – 4:6 *God is love;* and the test of true sonship to Him is, as before, the threefold evidence of:

    2:28 – 3:10   (i) Practical righteousness.

    3:11–18   (ii) Brotherly love.

    3:19–24   Digression on assurance.

    4:1–6   (iii) Confession that Jesus Christ is come in the flesh.

4:7 – 5:12 *God is love;* and the test of our dwelling in Him, and His dwelling in us is, as before:

    4:7–21   (i) Mutual love.

    5:1–3   (ii) The keeping of God's commandments.

    5:4–12   (iii) Belief that Jesus is the Son of God.

5:13–21 Conclusion. Five Christian certainties.

Analysis of 2 John

1–3   Opening salutation.

4–11   Message.

12, 13   Conclusion.

Analysis of 3 John

1–8   The message to Gaius.

9, 10   Diotrephes condemned.

11, 12   Demetrius approved.

13, 14   Conclusion.

☐   **STUDY 1   1 John 1:1 – 2:2**

1   To what unique experience in his life is the writer referring in verses 1–4? How does he describe it? *Cf.* Jn. 1:14. To what inestimable privilege did it lead him, and why does he want to make it known? *Cf.* 1 Thes. 3:8, 9.

2   The nature of God determines the conditions of fellowship with Him. See verses 6–10. How has He made fellowship with Himself possible for sinful man? What is His provision to enable fellowship to be maintained, and to meet failure if it should occur? If men deny in one way or another their need of this provision, what may we conclude concerning them? See verses 6, 8, 10.

Note. 1:5. 'Light': used in Scripture in various meanings, as signifying truth, goodness, joy, safety, life; just as 'darkness', on the contrary, denotes falsehood, evil, sorrow, peril, death. Here, 'light' signifies perfect truth and goodness, without any vestige of evil.

☐ **STUDY 2 1 John 2: 3-27**

1 Verses 3-11. If a man claims to know God, to abide in Christ and to be in the light, what must be his attitude to (a) Christ's word and commandment; (b) the example of Christ's life on earth; (c) fellow-Christians?

2 Verses 18-29. Amid false teachers and defection, what three safeguards for continuance in the faith does John give? See especially verses 24-27. If a professing Christian falls away from the truth, what is proved thereby which, before the falling away, may not have been at all obvious?

3 Verses 15-17. With what two arguments does John support the commandment of verse 15? How may this commandment be reconciled with Jn. 3:16?

Notes
1 Verse 7. *Cf.* Jn. 13:34, 35; 15:12.
2 Verse 8. John calls the old commandment new, both because Jesus Christ, by His teaching and living, has invested the old idea with a richer and deeper meaning, and because experimental Christianity is always new in kind or character.
3 Verse 15. 'The world': here it denotes human society as an ordered whole, considered both apart from, and in opposition to, God.

☐ **STUDY 3 1 John 2: 28 – 3: 10**

We enter today upon the second section of the Epistle (see Analysis).

1 2:28 – 3:3. The apostle, having begun in verse 29 to show that the test of sonship is righteousness of life, is carried away by the marvel of the new birth into a rapturous outburst of wonder and joy. Whence comes our sonship? How does the world regard it? What will be its future glory? How should this affect us now? *Cf.* Col. 3:4, 5.

2 3:4-9. These verses resume and expand the truth of 2:29. What five reasons are given to show that sinning is utterly incompatible with being a child of God?

Notes
1 2:28. This verse gives clear proof that John, no less than Paul and Peter, believed in the Lord's second coming. See also 3:2; 4:17.

2 2: 29. 'Born of him': the first reference to sonship in this letter.

3 3: 6, 9. These verses do not mean that a Christian is incapable of sinning, nor that one sin is proof of an unregenerate nature, but that it is impossible for a true child of God to persist in habitual sin.

☐ **STUDY 4** 1 John 3: 11 – 4: 6

1 3: 11–18. By what various arguments does John show, in verses 11–15, that mutual love is the essential mark of the children of God and that hatred is inadmissible? After what manner should we love? See verses 16–18 and *cf.* Jn. 15: 12; Eph. 5: 1, 2.

2 3: 19–24. A digression on the subject of assurance before God. The apostle first considers the case of a Christian whose heart condemns him. How is such a person to be reassured? See verses 19, 20. *Cf.* Heb. 6: 9, 10. Next the apostle considers the case of a Christian whose heart does not condemn him, because he is practising all the characteristics of a truly Christian life—obedience, love and faith. What blessings does this man enjoy? See verses 21–24.

3 What two tests are given here by which to know whether a prophet is, or is not, speaking by the Spirit of God? See especially 4: 2 and 6; see also Note 2 below.

Notes

1 3: 14. *Cf.* Jn. 5: 24. This gives the practical test whether a professed faith in Christ is genuine. *Cf.* Gal. 5: 6b; Jas. 2: 15–17.

2 4: 6. 'We are of God': the pronoun 'we' in the first half of this verse refers primarily, as in 1: 1–3, to John as representing the apostles, while not excluding those who, following after them, base their teaching upon the apostolic foundation.

☐ **STUDY 5** 1 John 4: 7 – 5: 3

We now begin the third section of the Epistle (see Analysis).

1 4: 7–10. What arguments are used in verses 7 and 8 to show that true Christians must love one another? In verses 9 and 10 the apostle speaks of the manifestation of God's love in Christ. How does he describe the gift? What does he say of its purpose? By what means was this purpose achieved, and for whom did God do this?

2 4: 11–18. The apostle goes over the same ground as before, but at a higher level. How does he here describe the Christian's relationship to God? How does he show that no higher or closer relationship can be conceived? Out of the depths of that relationship, the believer bears his testimony through the Spirit (verses 13–16; *cf.* Jn. 15: 26, 27).

3 4: 19 – 5: 3. In view of Mt. 22: 36, 37 why does not the apostle say in verse 11, 'Beloved, if God so loved us, we ought also to love God'? Why does John say, 'We ought also to love *one another*'? What other test of our love for God is also mentioned?

Notes
1 4: 17, 18. 'Because as he is . . .': *cf.* Jn. 3: 35 with 16: 27. Those who are loved of the Father need not look forward with dread. If we are still afraid, the remedy is to concentrate more upon the love of God shown in the cross and the resurrection.
2 5: 1. Faith in Jesus as the Christ implies receiving Him as such, and to receive Him is to be born of God (Jn. 1: 12, 13).

☐ **STUDY 6   1 John 5: 4–21**

1 The apostle has already given a warning against the subtle attraction of the world (see 2: 15–17). Now he reveals how the world may be conquered. Who does he say will overcome the world, and by what means? See verses 4–6; see also Note 1 below.

2 A faith that can effect such great results must be well attested. What fivefold witness is given in verses 7–11, and what marvellous fact does the witness attest?

3 Verses 13–20. There are here five great certainties concerning which John says 'We know'. What are they? Are you building your life upon this foundation?

Notes
1 Verse 6. This verse probably refers to our Lord's baptism and death, and not to Jn. 19: 34. He came not only to call us to repentance by the witness of His baptism, but also to wash away our sins with His blood. The two sacraments of the Christian church are the standing memorials of these things.
2 Verses 9 and 10. God has spoken to man in Jesus with the utmost clarity and finality. He that believes has an inward witness: he that believes not makes God a liar.
3 Verse 16. 'A mortal sin': *i.e.*, the deliberate, purposeful choice of darkness in preference to light.
4 Verse 21. 'Idols': anyone professing to worship God, but who denies that Jesus is the Son of God, is worshipping a false God. 'Be on your guard against all such idols' is John's final word.

☐ **STUDY 7   2 and 3 John**

1 Compare the tests of a true Christian found in 2 John with those given in 1 John.

2 Consider the three men mentioned in 3 John, all professing Christians. What does the apostle praise in Gaius? What faults does he find in Diotrephes? What threefold witness does he give in praise of Demetrius?

3   What dangers arise from listening to false teachers? What is John's answer to the claims of 'advanced thought'? See Note 3.

Notes
1   2 Jn. 2. *Cf.* NEB, 'whom I love in truth . . . for the sake of the truth'.
2   2 Jn. 4. 'Following the truth . . .': *i.e.*, living true Christian lives in obedience to the command which we have received from the Father.
3   2 Jn. 9. 'Goes ahead': *i.e.*, claims a knowledge superior to God's revelation.
4   3 Jn. 5. *Cf.* Heb. 13 : 2.

ISAIAH 40 - 66

☐   **STUDY 22   Isaiah 40**

The prophecies of chapters 40–48 have as their main theme the proclamation that God is about to restore the exiled Jews in Babylon to their own land. See Introduction. They refer to a time when the words spoken to Hezekiah (39 : 5–7) have been fulfilled. The first eleven verses are a prologue in which the prophet hears heavenly voices declaring to Jerusalem the glad message of redemption.

1   In verses 1–11 what four great facts are proclaimed by God to give comfort to His people? How does this prophecy of the future coming and glory of the Lord find fulfilment in the New Testament? *Cf.* Mt. 3 : 3; 1 Pet. 1 : 23–25; Jn. 10 : 11.

2   In verses 12–26 how is God shown to be beyond the petty mind of man to comprehend or to explain? How may we, as His creatures, draw on His infinite strength and power? See verses 29–31.

☐   **STUDY 23   Isaiah 41**

In this magnificent chapter the supremacy of the God of Israel is further demonstrated. First the nations (verses 1, 2) and then their gods (verses 21–29) are summoned before Him, and challenged as to what counsel they can give, and what control they can exercise in regard to the world-shaking onward march of Cyrus. They know nothing and can do nothing. It is the holy One of Israel who alone can predict the future, for He has planned all, and brought it to pass. Let Israel lift up his head, for he is God's elect and for him He has great purposes in view (verses 8–20).

1   The nations in their fear make new idols (verses 5–7). How are these idols shown to be worthless (verses 23, 24, 28, 29)? The reference in verses 2 and 25 is to Cyrus; what is God's relation to this mighty conqueror, and to the events of history in general (verses 2–4, 25–27)?

2   Tabulate the promises made to Israel in verses 8–20. How far and in what sense are they true for us today? *Cf.* 2 Cor. 1: 20. In what measure have we tried and proved God's promises?

Notes
1   Verses 2, 3. Here the first actor is God, and the second Cyrus.
2   Verses 21–24. The idols are now summoned before God. Note how they are challenged.

☐   **STUDY 24   Isaiah 42: 1 – 43: 13**

In chapter 41 Isaiah has shown that God has great purposes for Israel, His servant. That purpose is now declared. It is a purpose of blessing to all nations (42: 1–4 and 5–9; *cf.* Gn. 12: 3b). In order to accomplish it, God will redeem His people from their present plight (42: 13–16), confounding those that trust in idols (42: 17), and calling forth from far and near a paeon of praise to His Name (42: 10–12). Israel's present condition, under God's chastisement for her sins, is indeed pitiable (42: 18–25), but God will ransom His people, letting other nations suffer subjection in their stead (43: 1–7), and Israel shall then bear witness before the assembled nations to Jehovah's sovereign might and glory (43: 8–13).

1   42: 1–4. The prophet, in this picture of God's ideal Servant, perfectly portrays the Lord Jesus. *Cf.* Mt. 12: 18–21. What is said concerning (a) His relation to God; (b) His equipment for His task; (c) the purpose and scope of His mission; (d) the qualities that characterize Him; (e) the method of His ministry; (f) His endurance; (g) the final fulfilment of His work?

2   What does God promise to do for His people Israel in their distress (42: 16, 17; 43: 1–7)? What witness will Israel, when redeemed, bear to God and His saving power (43: 10–13)? Have we a similar testimony to the world around us concerning the reality of God's work of redemption?

Notes
1   42: 19. 'Blind': *i.e.*, to destiny and mission.
2   43: 3, 4. The meaning seems to be that God will give to Cyrus other people to serve him in payment for setting the Jews free.

☐ **STUDY 25   Isaiah 43: 14 – 44: 23**

In making reference to Babylon's impending downfall (43 : 14, 15) God answers an unspoken objection that such a thing is incredible. 'Do you not remember what I did at the Red Sea?' He asks (43 : 16, 17). 'Yet what I am about to do now is greater still' (43 : 18–21). He answers, too, a deeper cause of their unbelief, namely, a guilty conscience (43 : 21–24). 'I know it all,' He says, 'but I will pardon all' (43 : 25). 'My purpose toward you is one of blessing' (44 : 1–5).

1   What was the new thing that God was about to do, greater even than His deliverance of Israel at the Red Sea? *Cf.* chapter 35. What application has it to ourselves?

2   How does 43 : 22–28 show that Israel was not justified by works, but only by free grace? *Cf.* Rom. 3 : 23, 24. What further gift had God in store for His redeemed people, and what blessings will it bring (44 : 3–5)? *Cf.* Jn. 7 : 37–39.

3   What is the effect of idolatry on the mind of the worshipper? See 44 : 18–20. Have you realized the greatness of our privilege in knowing the true God? See 44 : 6–8.

Notes
1   43 : 22–24. During the exile, God had not burdened them with demands for sacrifice and offering. But they had burdened Him with their sins.
2   43 : 27, 28. 'Your first father': a reference probably to Jacob; *cf.* 48 : 1. 'Your mediators' may refer to priests and prophets; *cf.* Je. 2 : 8.

☐ **STUDY 26   Isaiah 44: 24 – 45: 25**

Allusion has already been made to Cyrus, but not by name (41 : 2, 25). Now he is directly and personally addressed, as one whom God has chosen as an instrument of His purpose of good towards Israel, and the purpose for which he has been raised up is declared (44 : 24 – 45 : 8). Those who object to this view of God's relation to Cyrus are rebuked (45 : 9–13), and there follows a remarkable prophecy of universal acknowledgment of the God of Israel as the one God, in whom alone is salvation (45 : 14–25).

1   What is said in 44 : 24 – 45 : 8 concerning (a) God's power in creation and in human history; (b) Cyrus, and what God will do for him and through him? What assurance should such a passage afford us?

2   What is the twofold answer given in 45 : 9–13 to those who question God's purposes and ways? *Cf.* Rom. 9 : 20. Are you ever guilty of feeling resentment against God?

3   In 45 : 14–25 what are the reasons given for the turning of men of all nations from their idols to the worship of the one true God? How does this anticipate the universal scope of Christ's redemption? *Cf.* Rom. 1 : 16.

Notes
1   44: 28. 'Shepherd': used frequently with the meaning of 'ruler'.
2   45: 13. 'Not for price or reward': this seems to contradict 43: 3, 4, but that passage speaks of the reward God gave, this of Cyrus' motive.
3   45: 14–17. Spoken to Israel. Verses 14b, 15 are the confession of the nations mentioned in verse 14.

☐   **STUDY 27   Isaiah 46 and 47**

These two chapters concern Babylon, the first showing the impotence of Babylon's gods and the folly of worshipping them (46: 1–7), and rebuking those Jews who would not receive God's revelation of His purposes (46: 8–13); and the second depicting Babylon as a proud queen humbled to the position of a menial slave, with none to help her.

1   Observe the difference in 46: 1–4 between the gods of Babylon that have to be borne by beasts, and carried away by their worshippers, and the God of Israel who bears His people throughout their history. Is your religion one that is a burden to you, or do you know One who will bear you even to old age?

2   What sins brought about Babylon's downfall, and God's judgment upon her? What did she assume was her security against future disaster (47: 8–13)?

3   What is the attitude of the Word of God to all forms of fortune-telling, crystal-grazing, and the like? What may we learn from chapter 47 about what will happen in the hour of judgment if we have been trusting in any other than in God?

Notes
1   46: 1, 2. The inhabitants of Babylon laid their chief idols (Bel and Nebo) on beasts, and carried them away in their flight.
2   47: 6. 'I profaned my heritage': *i.e.*, allowed the holy land to be defiled by foreign conquerors.

☐   **STUDY 28   Isaiah 48**

There seems to have been a party among the exiles which received God's message concerning Cyrus with disfavour. God has already rebuked them more than once (45: 9–13; 46: 12, 13); and now in verses 1–11 of this chapter He answers an objection they seem to have raised that the teaching was novel, and not in accord with God's usual procedure. He tells them that in spite of their rebellious attitude, He will carry out His plans.

1   What does God condemn in the nominal religiosity of the Jews? Why did this cause God to announce His intentions beforehand (verses 3–5), and yet to keep some of His purposes hidden (verses 7, 8)? Do we grieve God by failing to acknowledge Him, and to give Him glory?

2 Verses 17–22. What conditions does God lay down before we can experience the fullness of His grace and peace in our lives?

Notes
1 Verses 3–6a. 'The former things': a reference to prophecies long foretold and now fulfilled; see also verse 5a. In verse 6b God acknowledges that He has now used a different method, keeping back the revelation of His intended action until just before it happened, but in this also He had a purpose (verse 7).
2 Verse 10. 'But not like silver': a phrase that seems to express the divine sorrow that the refining process had not given a better result, such as happens when silver is refined. *Cf.* Je. 6: 29, 30.
3 Verse 14. 'All of you' refers to Israel; 'who among them' to the nations; and 'the Lord loves him' to Cyrus.

☐ **STUDY 29   Isaiah 49: 1 – 50: 3**

In chapters 40–48 the prophet has been concerned to show the supremacy of the God of Israel over the nations and their gods, and that God's purpose is to be accomplished through Cyrus. These two themes now disappear, and attention is turned to Israel's glorious future. Much of the section 49–55 consists of words of encouragement, spoken to overcome the doubts, hesitations and difficulties which the message of the preceding chapters had aroused in many minds. It contains also three of the 'Servant' passages in which the mission, the sufferings, and the atoning death of the Lord's Servant are set forth. (See Analysis.)

1 Verses 1–6. The 'Servant' speaks to the nations. What does he say concerning (a) his call; (b) his equipment; (c) his initial non-success, and his attitude in face of this; (d) the new task which God gave him to do? Although the passage applies to the Lord Jesus Christ, Paul uses part of it of himself and Barnabas. See Acts 13: 47. How is this? Have we then a share in the Servant's task? *Cf.* Jn. 20: 21.

2 How does the Lord answer Zion's doubts, first that the Lord has forsaken her (49: 14); second, that her children are taken from her and lost to her (49: 21); third, that Babylon was too strong to give up its prey (49: 24); and fourth, that her covenant relation with Jehovah is broken (50:1)?

3 Try to put yourself in the position of Israel in exile, as described in 49: 7a (*cf.* 41: 14, 'worm'); and then contemplate the faith that could see and declare the transformation announced in 49: 7b–13. On what is the prophet's faith founded? With verse 7 *cf.* Ps. 22: 6 and 27–29a.

Notes
1 49: 12. See mg. Some scholars connect 'Sinim' with China, but it seems unlikely that Jewish exiles would have travelled so far East by this period. The RSV 'Syene' refers to the more southerly country mentioned in Ezk. 29: 10; 30: 6.

2   50: 1, 2. 'What writ of divorce did I ever hand to your mother?' (Moffatt). The meaning is that the breach between God and Zion and her children is not irreparable.

☐   **STUDY 30   Isaiah 50: 4 – 51: 16**

1   What qualities are revealed in this picture of God's Servant? Meditate on the fulfilment of these in Christ. *Cf.* Jn. 12: 49; Mt. 26: 67. Consider from His example and experience what you may count upon God to do for you, and on what conditions.

2   What comfort and encouragement for your own faith do you find in 51: 1–6? What divine reassurances are given to those who are frightened by the hostility of men (verses 7, 8, 12–16)?

☐   **STUDY 31   Isaiah 51: 17 – 52: 12**

1   Consider the seeming hopelessness of Zion's condition in 51: 17–20, 23. How and why does God promise to act on her behalf (51: 22; 52: 3–6)? What must she herself do (52: 1, 2)? What message has this for a backsliding Christian? *Cf.* 1 Jn. 1: 9.

2   Let your imagination picture the joy of Zion described in 52: 7–12. What application does the apostle Paul make of this passage in Rom. 10: 14, 15 and 2 Cor. 6: 17?

Notes
1   51: 23. An allusion to the practice of making captives lie face downward on the ground, and using their backs as a road to walk on.
2   52: 8. 'Eye to eye': *i.e.*, face to face. This is how they will see the Lord when He returns to Zion.

☐   **STUDY 32   Isaiah 52: 13 – 53: 12**

This is the fourth of the 'Servant' passages, which portray with such marvellous accuracy the mission, character, and redemptive work of the Lord Jesus Christ. (See Introduction and Analysis.) Today's portion falls into three parts: (1) an introductory summary, announcing the Servant's exaltation after extreme suffering, and the effect of this upon surrounding nations and kings (52: 13–15); (2) the story of His life and suffering unto death, told by His now penitent fellow-countrymen (53: 1–9); and (3) the glorious issue, both for Himself and others, of His sufferings and redemptive work (53: 10–12).

1   How is God's Servant the Lord Jesus Christ depicted in 52: 13–15? Notice the depth of His suffering, His exaltation, and the effect of this upon the nations. *Cf.* 49: 7; Jn. 19: 1–5; Eph. 1: 20, 21.

2   Work out in detail the many close parallels between 53: 1–9 and the actual life of the Lord Jesus, as, for example, (a) the form of His

manifestation to the world; (b) the reception accorded Him; (c) His sufferings and the meaning of them; (d) His behaviour when arrested; (e) the manner of His death and of His burial.

3 Who are the 'offspring' spoken of in 53: 10, and what benefits are shown in this whole passage to have been procured for them by the Servant's substitutionary death? *Cf.* Heb. 2: 10. Do you belong to this number?

Notes
1 53: 1. The nations had not heard (52: 15); but Israel, hearing, had not believed.
2 53: 8. 'Considered': or possibly 'complained', in the sense of making an appeal against the sentence. All were indifferent and even scornful. *Cf.* Mt. 27: 39–44.
3 53: 11. 'By his knowledge' may mean 'by means of His knowledge' or 'by the knowledge of Him' (on the part of others). *Cf.* Jn. 17: 3.

☐ **STUDY 33 Isaiah 54**

1 In verses 4–10 consider all the reasons given why God's reconciled people should not fear. In what ways will God be like a 'husband' to His people (verse 4–7)? How does God reveal in His treatment of His people that He is faithful to His covenants (verses 9, 10)?

2 'This is the heritage', says the prophet, 'of the servants of the Lord' (verse 17). What is this inheritance? List the blessings here promised. What guarantees that we can enjoy them?

3 William Carey applied verses 2 and 3 to the missionary enterprise, and summoned the church to reach out to the unevangelized nations. What does this chapter mean for you? In what direction does it summon you to 'lengthen your cords and strengthen your stakes'? Have you grasped how great your God is, how far-reaching His purposes of blessing?

☐ **STUDY 34 Isaiah 55**

1 Is the appeal in this chapter any less applicable or less urgent in our day than it was to the Jews living in Babylon? Are you then proclaiming it to those around you? Try to state its argument in present-day language.

2 In verses 8–13 what do we learn about (a) man's inability to comprehend God; (b) God's word of promise; (c) the future for God's people? How ought we to act in response to such truths?

☐ STUDY 35 Isaiah 56 and 57

The good tidings of Jehovah's purpose to bring back the exiles and to restore Jerusalem produced many repercussions among different classes of hearers. In the opening verses of today's portion the prophet replies to the questionings of two special groups: (1) non-Jews, who had joined themselves to Israel (56: 3a, 6–8), and (2) eunuchs, who feared God (56: 3b–5). Might they also participate in the promised deliverance? The Lord's answer is that if they fulfilled the conditions of the covenant, they would be welcome to a full share in its blessings. In 56: 9 – 57: 14 the prophet rebukes two other groups: the leaders of the community in Jerusalem (56: 9–12), and those who were openly practising idolatry (57: 1–14). There follows a striking description of the kind of persons with whom God will dwell, and of His purposes of grace towards His people (57: 15–21).

1 What were the spiritual conditions on which the Lord would recognize a man, whether a Jew or not, as being one of His own people? See 56: 1–8. How does this anticipate the New Testament offer of the gospel to all, and how does it fall short of it? With verse 7 *cf.* Mt. 21: 13; and with verse 8 *cf.* Jn. 10: 16.

2 What do these two chapters, and more particularly 57: 15–21, teach us about God?

3 Consider the sad picture in 56: 9 – 57: 14 of a community whose leaders were unworthy, and whose members were forsaking the Lord for idols. What warnings for ourselves may be found in it?

Notes
1 56: 3b–5. In the new community physical and racial disabilities would no longer be a ground of exclusion. *Cf.* Dt. 23: 1, 3–8.
2 56: 10. 'Watchmen': *i.e.*, the leaders of the community, also called 'shepherds' (verse 11). They loved ease, gain, and drunken carnivals.
3 57: 3. A reference to their idolatrous practices; so also in verses 7, 8.
4 57: 11. 'You went on fearlessly, in faithlessness, giving no thought to me, in your indifference. Is it not so? I said no word, I hid my face from you, and on you went, fearing me not' (Moffatt).

☐ STUDY 36 Isaiah 58

1 Has fasting itself any value in God's sight? What does He look for in His people, and why is such conduct called 'fasting'? In verses 8–12, what promises of spiritual blessing does God give to those who are right in spirit towards Himself and their fellowmen?

2 Examine your own attitude to Sunday in the light of verses 13, 14.

Notes
1 Verse 4. 'You fast only to quarrel and to fight . . .' Fasting, if not done in the right spirit, is apt to make men irritable and contentious, quick to use their fist.

2 Verse 9. 'The pointing of the finger': probably a gesture of haughty contempt.

3 Verse 13. 'If you turn back your foot from the sabbath': *i.e.*, regard it as holy ground, not to be profaned by common business. *Cf.* 56:2; Ne. 13:15–21.

☐ **STUDY 37 Isaiah 59**

This chapter in its opening verses is an exposure of the sins that separate from God (verses 1–8). In verses 9–15a the people describe their sorrowful state, and make confession. But they feel that if action on God's part is to be for ever restrained by their sinfulness the position seems hopeless indeed (see Note 2 on 'justice' below). Then in the closing verses of the chapter comes the triumphant divine answer (verses 15b–21). God is not baffled, and when there is no human help He Himself comes to the rescue, in judgment upon evil-doers on the one hand, and in redemption for the penitent on the other.

1 Verses 1–15. What various sins are mentioned here, and what are the consequences in the personal, social and spiritual life of the people? With verses 1, 2 *cf.* 1:15–17; Mi. 3:4.

2 What is the motive of God's intervention, as described in verses 15b–21? What is its twofold purpose, and what its world-wide issue? When does St. Paul look for this to be fulfilled to Israel (Rom. 11:25–27)? Yet, for us who believe on Jesus Christ, is it not in part fulfilled to us now, and not least verse 21? *Cf.* Jn. 14:16, 26.

Notes
1 Verses 5, 6. The plan and plots of evil-doers working fresh evil, and giving no useful result.
2 Verse 9. The word 'justice' is used in these verses in two senses, (a) as right done by man (verse 8, 15b), and (b) as divine judgment, exercised on behalf of Israel against her oppressors (verses 9, 11, 14). The people's lament was that the latter was withheld, because the former was lacking.

☐ **STUDY 38 Isaiah 60**

An inspired vision of Zion, when God shall have fulfilled towards her all His purpose, and clothed her with His glory.

1 Try to build up the picture of the glorified Zion as given in this vision. Gather out the references to God, and observe carefully the place He occupies in Zion. Has He this central place in your life, and in your Christian fellowship?

2 Consider how many of the features of beauty and glory in the Zion of this chapter are to be found, in their spiritual counterpart, in a life dwelling in the fullness of the Holy Spirit. See especially verses 2, 5, 7 (last clause), 13 (last clause), 16b, and 17–21; and *cf.* 2 Cor. 3:18; 4:6; 6:16; Eph. 3:14–21.

Notes

1   Verses 8, 9. The ships coming from the west, with their white sails, looking like a flock of doves.

2   Verse 13. 'The place of my sanctuary': *i.e.*, the Temple, called also 'the place of my feet'.

3   Verse 21. 'That I might be glorified': compare 'he has glorified you' (verse 9) and 'I will glorify my glorious house' (verse 7; so also verse 13). Where God is glorified, all else is glorified in Him. *Cf.* 2 Thes. 1: 12.

☐   **STUDY 39   Isaiah 61: 1 – 63: 6**

1   How would you summarize the teaching of chapters 61 and 62 regarding the Lord's purpose of good for Zion? What do we learn, for example, about (a) the relation to God into which God's people will be brought (61: 6, 8, 9; 62: 4, 12), and (b) the response of God's people to His promised salvation (61: 10)? Is your experience of this kind?

2   In chapter 61 the coming salvation is proclaimed, in 62 it is prayed for (verses 1, 6, 7). If the gospel is to prevail on earth, are not both the proclamation of it and prayer concerning it still necessary? *Cf.* Rom. 10: 14, 15; 2 Thes. 3: 1. What characteristic of prevailing prayer is emphasized here?

3   In Lk. 4: 17–21 our Lord says that the opening words of chapter 61 were spiritually fulfilled in His own ministry. Why did He cut His reading in the synagogue short in the middle of 61: 2? Meditate on the scope of our Lord's ministry as revealed in these verses.

Notes

1   62: 2. 'A new name': the symbol both of a new character, and of a new relation to God. *Cf.* Rev. 2: 17; 3: 12.

2   63: 4. The day of redemption is also a day of judgment. *Cf.* 61: 2; Jn. 3: 17–19.

☐   **STUDY 40   Isaiah 63: 7 – 64: 12**

1   63: 7–14. How does the suppliant begin his prayer? What has Israel learnt of God's mercy and love in her past? What lesson is there here for us when in our need we pray to God? *Cf.* Eph. 1: 16; Phil. 1: 3; 4: 6; Col. 1: 3.

2   What five pleas are found in 63: 15–19? In 64: 4, 5, the suppliant begins to advance another plea. What is it, and why is he unable to continue it (verses 6, 7)? Do you know how to plead with God? What pleas may we rightly make?

Notes

1   63: 10, 11, 14. The references to the Holy Spirit in this prayer are strikingly clear and full.

2   63: 17a. The prolonging of the suffering was tending to increase the ungodliness.

☐   **STUDY 41   Isaiah 65**

1   Verses 1–7. What picture of God is unfolded in verses 1 and 2? *Cf.* Mt. 7: 2. Why has He been unable to answer the prophet's prayer for Israel's salvation? *Cf.* 59: 1–3. How does God purpose to deal with them (verses 8–12)?

2   What is to be the lot of God's chosen people in Jerusalem in the new age that is to dawn (verses 17–25)? What in contrast is going to be the life and end of those who forsake God (verses 11–15)?

Notes

1   Verses 3–7. A condemnation of various idolatrous practices.

2   Verse 8. 'When a bunch of grapes holds some good wine, men say, "Destroy it not, it holds a blessing" ' (Moffatt). So God will save the good in Israel.

3   Verse 11. 'Fortune' and 'Destiny': the Hebrew words are Gad and Meni, the names of two gods.

☐   **STUDY 42   Isaiah 66**

The distinction is maintained between those who are disobedient to God, and those who fear Him. The final destiny of the two classes is made clear. God will thus be fully and finally glorified. *Cf.* 2 Thes. 1: 7–12.

1   When God looks down upon men's worship, what is it He values? See verses 1–4; *cf.* Ps. 51: 17; Jn. 4: 23, 24.

2   What is the end of those who, having heard God's voice, will not give heed? See especially verses 4, 5, 6, 17, 24. What, on the other hand, is promised to Zion and her children? See verses 7–14, 20–22. While these promises are made primarily to Jerusalem and are yet to be fulfilled, they also declare the spiritual good things which God has provided for us in His Son, and which we may claim for ourselves in Him. *Cf.* Rom. 8: 16, 17, 32; 1 Cor. 3: 22; 2 Cor. 1: 20.

3   How does the prophet's vision of God's purpose for the nations fall short of the glory of the full revelation of this 'mystery' in the New Testament?